Berlitz®

Malaysia

Front cover: Beach hut, Sabah

Below: Blue Mosque, Shah Alam

TOP 10 ATTRACTIONS

Burau Bay One of many beautiful beaches that Langkawi Island has to offer sunlovers *(page 81)*

Petronas Twin Towers The world's tallest pair of buildings are a striking sight on Kuala Lumpur's skyline *(page 38)*

Blue Mosque •
This spectacular Islamic landmark is an easy day trip from KL *(page 41)*

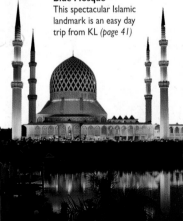

Batu Caves A vast network of limestone caves transformed into a Hindu shrine *(page 43)*

Visiting an Iban longhouse An experience not to be missed when travelling in the state of Sarawak *(page 111)*

George Town Its architecture ranges from colonial to Chinese *(page 69)*

Taman Negara A national park of ancient rainforests and river rapids *(page 55)*

Sepilok Orang-Utan Sanctuary Prepares once captive and orphaned animals for life in the wild *(page 128)*

Kinabalu Park Superb scenery and fascinating flora and fauna make it a major attraction in Sabah *(page 123)*

Mount Api's Pinnacles A mesmerising sight in Mount Mulu National Park *(page 118)*

CONTENTS

39

86

122

147

40
130

Features

INTRODUCTION

As Malaysia continues resolutely into the modern age, it remains, culturally and historically, a rich, multi-layered blend of traditions fuelled by a modern, busy and outward-looking economy. From sandy beaches, broad brown rivers and deep forests, to rising skyscrapers and wide expressways, Malaysia is set to exceed visitors' expectations.

Visitors see the traditional juxtaposed with the modern among Chinatown shophouses, in the vibrancy of night markets, and even in the modern shopping centres. They see great architectural splendour among the many mosques, Chinese and Hindu shrines, and even the Petronas Twin Towers of Kuala Lumpur. The ways of the past can be felt amid the longhouses of Sabah and Sarawak, in the kite-flying and top-spinning traditions of Kelantan and Terengganu, and in the evocative colours of batik art.

Your gateway to Malaysia will probably be through its capital, Kuala Lumpur, a prosperous and modern city where mansions, mosques and temples are jostle with expressways and skyscrapers, with parks and gardens to balance the urban areas.

Situated in the heart of Southeast Asia, Malaysia is about the size of Japan and has a population of over 26

Facts and figures

Peninsular and East Malaysia together cover a total area of 329,759 sq km (127,317 sq miles). The peninsula is 750km (466 miles) long and about 350km (218 miles) at its widest point. It is only two-thirds the size of East Malaysia. Some four-fifths of Malaysia was originally covered by rainforest.

Of the many rivers, the peninsula's longest is the Pahang, at 475km (295 miles). In East Malaysia, the longest river is the Rejang, at 563km (350 miles).

The Petronas Towers, KL

million. The country is divided into two major regions: the peninsula, bordered by Thailand, the Strait of Malacca and the South China Sea; and East Malaysia, whose two states, Sabah and Sarawak, are located on the island of Borneo, 800km (500 miles) across the South China Sea. Sabah and Sarawak are vast regions of forests, rivers and mountains bordering the Indonesian state of Kalimantan and the sultanate of Brunei. Industry and urban society are concentrated on the peninsula, especially on the west coast, while East Malaysia is dominated by rainforests. The two regions share a hot, humid climate, but differ greatly in their population density and urban development.

Malaysia's relative wealth is reflected in the excellent road and rail networks along the peninsula's west coast. Its per capita income is one of the highest in Southeast Asia.

Five Kinds of Forest

Variations in soil, slope and altitude give rise to five kinds of forest:

Mangrove forest. Mangrove trees and shrubs grow on coastal marshland in the brackish zone between the sea and fresh water. An associated species is the low, trunkless nipa palm, whose fronds have traditionally been used as roofing material for coastal huts.

Freshwater swamp. Abundant fruit trees in the fertile alluvium of river plains attract prolific wildlife. Where swamp gives way to dry land, you may see the fascinating, monstrous strangler-figs.

Dipterocarp forest. Named after the two-winged fruit borne by many of the forest's tallest trees, this dry-land rainforest is what you will see most frequently from just above sea level up to an altitude of 900m (3,000ft).

Heath forest. Poor soil on the flat terrain leading to foothills or on sandy mountain-ridges produces only low, stunted trees with thick leaves.

Montane forest. At 1,200m (4,000ft) and above in large mountain ranges, or as low as 600m (2,000ft) on small isolated mountains, the large trees and liana creepers give way to myrtle, laurel and oak trees.

Farmers cut terraces into hillsides to cultivate vegetables and tea

Nature's Supremacy

Whether you are staying at a beach resort or visiting a city, a stand of forest is never far away. Even in modern, urban Kuala Lumpur, a construction site abandoned too long to the tropical sun and rain will soon sprout a luxuriant growth of *lalang* grass.

The country's prosperity has come from its coastal plains, wider on the west than the east side of the peninsula. Malaysia rose first as a trading point for Asia and Europe, with the port of Melaka (or Malacca). Then came tin mining and rubber plantations and, more recently, palm oil, timber and petroleum and gas. Padifields in the northwest and around river deltas on the east coast are where Malaysia's rice is cultivated.

Mangrove swamps along the coast and nipa palms give rise to mangrove forests. The world's oldest rainforests engulf low but steeply rising mountain chains that cross the peninsula

Highland forest, Fraser's Hill

from east to west, with one long north–south Main Range as their backbone. Until the highway construction of the modern era, access to many forested areas had been – and sometimes still is – only by river.

In East Malaysia's states of Sarawak and Sabah, plantations alternate with marshland on the plains before giving way to the forests of the interior. To the south, a natural barrier of mountains forms the border with Indonesian Kalimantan. Near the coast at the northern end of the Crocker Range is Mount Kinabalu. At 4,101m (13,455ft), it is one of the highest peaks in Southeast Asia and popular with climbers.

With the growth of tourism, resort facilities have burgeoned in islands such as Penang, Pangkor and Langkawi on the west coast of the peninsula, Tioman on the east coast, and around Sabah's islands off Kota Kinabalu.

To go to Malaysia without setting foot in the rainforest would be to overlook one of the essential features of the country. Sounds flood in from all sides: the buzz of crickets, the chatter of squirrels, the cries of gibbons. Animal life may be harder to spot as, unlike the wildlife of the African plains, most animals of the Malaysian rainforest are not conspicuous. Tigers and leopards remain rare, and the elephants, rhinos, tigers and bears are the smallest of their kind.

Many and Diverse Peoples

Malaysia can be proud of the continued coexistence of the three prominent peoples of the nation: Malays (mostly Muslim), Chinese (mostly Buddhist) and Indians (mainly Hindu). Although there have been periods of social unrest in Malaysia's past, these people generally live in harmony, and it is not unusual to see a mosque, pagoda, temple and church all built close to each other. Another feature is the marvellous diversity in the nation's food, with food centres often serving Malay, Chinese and Indian dishes at adjacent stalls. The country's multiculturalism is also apparent in tribal communities like the Kadazan/Dusun of Sabah, the Iban of Sarawak *(see page 103)*, and the Orang Asli people who first arrived on the peninsula 10,000 years ago.

The Malays, or *Bumiputra* (meaning sons of the soil), make up over half the population and this is reflected in Islam's status as the national religion, with Malay – *Bahasa Malaysia* – as the national language.

The bulk of Malays are humble town- or village-dwelling people, tending goats and buffalo, growing rice, and working in the coconut, rubber, timber, rattan and bamboo industries. Just as court rituals are influenced by the ancient customs of pre-Muslim Malaya, so a mild Sunnite version of Islam is often seasoned with the ancient beliefs of animist medicine-men.

Religious Tolerance

To the outsider, public life in Malaysia may sometimes seem like one religious holiday after another. All the world's major beliefs, along with an array of minor ones, are practised in Malaysia. While Islam is the official religion, most other faiths are treated with a tolerance that contrasts with ethnic struggles at the political or economic level. The free pursuit of all beliefs is guaranteed by the constitution.

Useful phrases

Courtesy and knowledge of a little Bahasa Malaysia are always welcomed.
A simple phrase such as *terima kasih* (thank you) is likely to be answered *sama sama* (you're welcome). Other phrases can be found in the language section (see page 164), but just remembering *selamat pagi* (good morning) or *selamat tengah hari* (good afternoon) is worth the effort.

Islam is observed by some 52 percent of the population, mostly Malays, but also some Indians, Pakistanis and Chinese. First introduced by Arab and Indian Gujarati traders, its earliest trace is an inscribed 14th-century Terengganu stone. From 1400, the religion was spread through the peninsula by the Melaka sultanate. Today, each sultan or ruler serves as leader of the faith in his state. Since Islam makes no distinction between secular and religious spheres, it regulates many aspects of everyday life, from greeting people to washing and eating.

Now practised by 17 percent of the population, Buddhism was introduced to the peninsula by early Chinese and Indian travellers, but only took hold when Chinese traders came to Melaka in the 15th century. With their 3,500 temples, societies and community organisations, the Chinese practise the Mahayana (Greater Vehicle) form of Buddhism, which evolved in the first century BC. A more rigorous form, known as Hinayana (Lesser Vehicle), is practised by the Thais in Kelantan, Kedah, Perlis and Penang. For most Malaysian Chinese, the Confucian moral and religious system coexists with Buddhism.

As the country's earliest organised religion, pre-Islamic Hinduism of the Brahman priestly caste reinforced the authority of the Indian ruling class. Rituals of that era survive in Malay weddings and other ceremonies. Modern Hinduism in Malaysia has been shaped by 19th-century immigration from the Indian subcontinent. The largest contingent and most powerful influence were Tamil labourers from southern India and Sri

Lanka, with their devotion to Shiva. Temples have been built on almost every plantation worked by Indian labourers.

Christians make up 8 percent of Malaysia's population, mostly in Sabah and Sarawak. This is largely due to Catholic and Methodist missionary work from the 19th century onwards, although many of the Catholics are of Eurasian origin, dating back to the Portuguese colonisation of Melaka. Christmas is widely celebrated throughout the country and Easter is a public holiday in Sarawak and Sabah.

Despite its reputation for religious and multiracial harmony, Malaysia faces the challenge of maintaining stability. In the political sphere, rifts have deepened between fundamentalists and more moderate Muslims. Ethnic wealth gaps are also a problem. Nevertheless, Malaysia remains one of Southeast Asia's most successful economies, and attracts tourists with its diverse landscapes and and multicultural, welcoming population.

Cosmopolitan Kuala Lumpur bustles with a unique ethnic mix

A BRIEF HISTORY

Over the centuries, life in Malaysia has always been able to attract immigrants. Bountiful food sources may have made it an inviting place for the contemporaries of Java Man in 230,000BC. But thus far, the country's earliest traces of Homo sapiens, found in Sarawak's Niah Caves, are fragments of a skull dating to 40,000BC.

By 2,000BC, the nomadic Orang Asli people, hunting with bows and arrows, were driven back from the coasts by waves of immigrants arriving in outrigger canoes. Mongolians from South China and Polynesian and Malay peoples from the Philippines and the Indonesian islands settled along the rivers of the peninsula and northern Borneo. They practised a slash-and-burn agriculture of yams and millet, exhausting the soil and imposing a semi-nomadic existence from one forest clearing to another. Families lived in wooden longhouses like those still seen among the Ibans of Sarawak. Other migrants arrived and settled along the coasts – sailors, fishermen, traders and pirates – known euphemistically as *Orang Laut* (sea people).

Indian Influence

In the early centuries of the Christian era, the peninsula's advantageous position made it an ideal stop for trade with Bengal and southern India. It attracted Indianised colonies from the Mekong Valley of Indochina. Their rulers introduced Buddhism and Hinduism, Brahmin ministers to govern and an elaborate court ritual. What is now the state of Kedah benefited from the plough and other Indian farming practices. From its golden era, a 9th-century Hindu temple, the Candi Bukit Batu Pahat, has been restored at Mount Jerai. On the east coast in Terengganu and Kelantan, the weaving and metalwork still practised today originated from this early colonisation.

Srivijaya, the most powerful of the Indianised colonies and a centre of Buddhist learning, built a maritime empire from its base on Sumatra. With the *Orang Laut* pirates as allies, Srivijaya controlled the Strait of Malacca, a key link between the Indian Ocean and the South China Sea. Its colonies on the peninsula's west coast introduced the Malay language (*Malayu* was the name of a Sumatran state).

As Srivijaya declined in the 14th century, the Malay peninsula was carved up among Siam (now Thailand), Cambodia and the Javanese Hindu empire of Majpahit. Around 1400, fighting over the island of Singapore drove the Srivijaya prince Parameswara to seek refuge up the coast of the peninsula with his *Orang Laut* pirate friends in Melaka.

Rice is still harvested by hand in some parts of the country

The Glory of Melaka

The Chinese were the first to spot the strategic and commercial potential of Melaka – once an infertile, swampy plain – as a harbour sheltered from the monsoons, with a deep-water channel close to the coast. In 1409, under a directive from Emperor Chu Ti to pursue trade in the South Seas and Indian Ocean, a Chinese fleet headed by Admiral Cheng Ho called into Melaka. They made Parameswara an offer he could not refuse: port facilities and financial support

Melaka was once a busy trading port

in exchange for Chinese protection against the Siamese (Thais). In 1411, Parameswara took the money to Beijing himself, and the emperor gratefully made him a vassal king.

Twenty years later, however, the Chinese withdrew. The new ruler of Melaka, Sri Maharajah, had switched his allegiance to Muslim traders. Islam won its place in Malaya not by conquest, but by trade and peaceful preaching. Bengalis had already brought the faith to the east coast. In Melaka, and throughout the peninsula, Islam thrived as a strong, male-dominated religion, offering dynamic leadership and preaching brotherhood and self-reliance – all qualities ideally suited to the coastal trade. At the same time, Sufi mystics synthesised Islamic teaching with local Malay traditions of animistic magic and charisma, though Islam did not become the state religion until Muzaffar Shah became sultan of Melaka (1446–59).

Yet the key figure in the sultanate was Tun Perak, *bendahara* (prime minister) and military commander. He expanded

Melaka's power along the west coast and to Singapore and the Bintan Islands. He also had *Orang Laut* pirates patrolling the seas to extort tribute from passing ships. After allied district chiefs had repelled assaults from Siam-controlled armies from Pahang, Tun Perak led a celebrated victory over a Siamese fleet off Batu Pahat in 1456. To smooth things over, the sultan sent a peace mission to the Siamese court and an envoy to China, reconfirming Muzzafar Shah's title as most obedient vassal.

By 1500, Melaka was the leading port in Southeast Asia, drawing Chinese, Indian, Javanese and Arab merchants. Governed with diplomacy by the great *bendahara* Tun Mutahir, the sultanate asserted its supremacy over virtually the whole Malay Peninsula and across the Strait of Malacca to the east coast of Sumatra. Prosperity was based entirely on the entrepôt trade: importing textiles from India, spices from Indonesia, silk and porcelain from China, gold and pepper from Sumatra, camphor from Borneo and sandalwood from Timor.

Portuguese Conquest

In the 16th century, Melaka fell victim to Portugal's anti-Muslim crusade in the campaign to break the Arab-Venetian domination of commerce between Asia and Europe. The first visit of a Portuguese ship to Melaka in 1509 ended badly, as embittered Gujarati Indian merchants poisoned the atmosphere against the Portuguese. Two years later, the Portuguese sent their fleet, led by Afonso de Albuquerque, to seize Melaka. No match for the Portuguese invaders, the court fled south,

Afonso de Albuquerque

establishing a new centre of Malay Muslim power in Johor. Albuquerque built a fort and church on the site of the sultan's palace. He ruled the non-Portuguese community with Malay *kapitan* headmen and the foreigners' *shahbandar* harbour-masters. Relations were better with the merchants from China and India than with the Muslims.

The 130 years of Portuguese control proved precarious. They faced repeated assault from Malay forces, and malaria was a constant scourge. Unable or unwilling to court the old vassal Malay states or the *Orang Laut* pirates to patrol the seas, the new rulers forfeited their predecessors' monopoly in the Strait of Malacca and, with it, command of the Moluccas spice trade.

They made little effort, despite the Jesuit presence in Asia, to convert local inhabitants to Christianity or to expand their territory. The original colony of 600 men intermarried with local women to form a large Eurasian community.

Remnants of the A Famosa fort built by Afonso de Albuquerque

The Dutch Take Over

Intent on capturing a piece of the Portuguese trade in pepper and other spices, the Java-based Dutch joined the Malays in 1633 to blockade Melaka. This ended in a seven-month siege with the Portuguese surrender in 1641.

Buffalo horns

The name *Minangkabau* roughly means 'buffalo horns' and is reflected in the distinctive upward curving roofs in museums and government offices built in the Minangkabau style.

Unlike the Portuguese, the Dutch decided to do business with the Malays of Johor, who controlled the southern half of the peninsula together with Singapore and the Riau islands. Without ever regaining the supremacy of the old Melaka sultanate, Johor had become the strongest regional power. Meanwhile, fresh blood came in with the migration into the southern interior of Minangkabau farmers from Sumatra, while tough Bugis warriors from the east Indonesian Celebes (Sulawesi) roved across the peninsula. The Minangkabau custom of electing their leaders provided the model for rulership elections in modern federal Malaysia. Their confederation of states became today's Negeri Sembilan (Nine States), with Seremban as its capital.

In the 18th century, with the Dutch concentrating again on Java and the Moluccas, the Bugis took advantage of the vacuum by raiding Perak and Kedah, imposing their chieftains in Selangor and becoming the power behind the Johor throne.

British Rule

The British had shown little interest in Malaya. That changed in 1786, when the Sultan of Kedah granted Francis Light, a representative of the East India Company, rights to the island of Penang and the strip of mainland coast called Province Wellesley (now Seberang Perai) as a counterweight to the demands of the Siamese and Burmese. Unlike Portuguese and Dutch trading posts, Penang was declared a duty-free zone, attracting settlers and traders. By 1801, the population was over 10,000, concentrated in the island's capital, George Town.

In 1805, a dashing EIC administrator, Thomas Stamford Bingley Raffles, came to Penang at the age of 24. His knowledge of Malay customs and language, and humanitarian vision, made him vital in Britain's expanding role in Malay affairs. Raffles secured his place in history by negotiating, in 1819, the creation of the Singapore trading post with the Sultan of Johor. Singapore became capital of the Straits Settlements – as the EIC called its Malay holdings, incorporating Penang and Melaka – and was the linchpin of Britain's 150-year regional presence.

The Straits Settlements were formed after the Anglo-Dutch Treaty of London (1824). This colonial carve-up partitioned the Malay world through the Strait of Malacca. The peninsula and Sumatra, after centuries of common language, religion and traditions, were divided. The islands south of Singapore, including Java and Sumatra, went to the Dutch. Peninsular Malaysia and northwest Borneo remained under British control. From 1826, British law was technically in force, but in practice few British people lived in the Straits, and local affairs were run by merchant leaders serving as unofficial *kapitans*.

Apart from the few Malays in the settlements' rural communities of Province Wellesley and the Melaka hinterland, the majority still lived inland. Unity among them and the east coast communities trading with the Siamese, Indochinese and Chinese came from their shared rice economy, language, culture, and customs inherited from the Melaka sultanate.

Province Wellesley acted as a mainland buffer for Penang, and Melaka similarly turned its back on affairs in the hinterland. When Kedah and Perak sought British help against Siam, the British took the easier option of siding with the Siamese to quell revolts. But in the 1870s, under the Colonial Office, the profits gained from exporting Malayan tin through Singapore forced the British to take an active role in Malay affairs.

The lucrative tin mines of Kuala Lumpur, of Sungai Ujong (Negeri Sembilan), and of Larut and Taiping (Perak) were run for the Malay rulers by Chinese managers and labourers. Chinese secret societies waged gang wars for the control of the mines, bringing tin production to a halt at a time when world demand was at a peak. In 1874, Governor Andrew Clarke persuaded the Malay rulers of Perak and Selangor to accept British Residents as advisors; in return, Britain offered protection.

It began badly. Within a year the Resident in Perak, James Birch, was assassinated after efforts to impose direct British control. Subsequent British advisors served on a consultative state council alongside Malay ruler, chiefs and Chinese *kapitans*. Birch's successor in Perak, Hugh Low (1877–89), was more successful. Reforms he persuaded the ruler to accept included organising revenue collection, dismantling slavery and regulating land. Unity was enhanced by the growing network

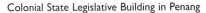

Colonial State Legislative Building in Penang

of railways and roads. Governor Frederick Weld (1880–87) extended the residency system to Negeri Sembilan and the more recalcitrant Pahang, where Sultan Wan Ahmad was forced to open the Kuantan tin mines to British prospectors.

A Federation of Malay States – Selangor, Perak, Negeri Sembilan and Pahang – was proclaimed in 1896 to coordinate economics and administration. Frank Swettenham became first Resident-General, with Kuala Lumpur as the capital.

The White Rajahs of Borneo

In the 19th century, Borneo remained undeveloped. Balanini pirates, fervent Muslims, disputed the coast of northeastern Borneo (modern-day Sabah) with the sultanate of Brunei. Sarawak's coast and interior were controlled by the Iban, Sea Dayak pirates and Land Dayak slash-and-burn farmers. The region's only major resource was the gold and antimony mined by the Chinese in the Sarawak River valley.

James Brooke, Rajah of Sarawak

In 1839, the Governor of Singapore sent James Brooke (1803–68) to promote trade with the Sultan of Brunei. In exchange for helping the regent end a revolt by Malay chiefs, Brooke was made Rajah of Sarawak in 1841, with his capital in Kuching. He tried to halt the Dayaks' piracy and head-hunting (believed to bring spiritual energy to their communities), while defending their more 'morally acceptable' customs. His attempts to limit the opium trade met with resistance from the Chinese in Bau, who revolted. His counter-attack with Dayak warriors drove the Chinese out of Bau. Thereafter, Chinese settlement was discouraged.

In 1863, Brooke retired, handing Sarawak over to his nephew, Charles. A better administrator and financier, Charles Brooke imposed his efficient lifestyle. He brought Dayak leaders onto his ruling council but favoured the colonial practice of divide and rule by pitting one tribe against another.

In 1877, northeast Borneo (Sabah) was 'rented' from the Sultan of Brunei by British businessman Alfred Dent, who was operating a royal charter for the British North Borneo Company. This region was grouped together with Sarawak and Brunei in 1888 as a British protectorate, named North Borneo.

The Early 20th Century

The British extended their control over the peninsula by putting together the whole panoply of colonial administration. At the same time, the tin industry, which had been dominated by the Chinese, passed increasingly into the hands of Westerners, who employed modern technology. Petroleum had been found in northern Borneo, at Miri, and in Brunei, and the Anglo-Dutch Shell company used Singapore for exporting.

But the major breakthrough for the Malay economy was rubber, developed by the director of Singapore Botanical Gardens, Henry Ridley. World demand increased with the motor car and electrical industries, and rocketed during World War I. By 1920, Malaya was producing 53 percent of the world's rubber. Together with effective control of the rubber and tin industries, the British firmly controlled government.

The census of 1931 was an alarm signal for the Malay national consciousness. Bolstered by an influx of immigrants to meet the rubber and tin booms, non-Malays now slightly outnumbered the indigenous population. The Depression of 1929 stepped up ethnic competition in the shrinking job market, and nationalism developed to safeguard Malay interests against the Chinese and Indians rather than British imperialism.

Conservative Muslim intellectuals and community leaders came together at the Pan-Malayan Malay Congress in Kuala Lumpur in 1939. The following year, they were joined in Singapore by representatives from Sarawak and Brunei.

Japanese Occupation

The Pacific War actually began on Malaysia's east coast. On 8 December 1941, an hour before Pearl Harbor was bombed, Japanese troops landed on Sabak Beach *(see page 87)*. Japan coveted Malaya's natural resources of rubber, tin and oil and the port of Singapore. The stated aim of the Japanese invasion was a 'Greater East Asia Co-Prosperity Sphere', appealing to Malay nationalism to throw off Western imperialism.

Not expecting a land attack, Commonwealth troops on the peninsula were ill-prepared. The landings were launched from bases ceded to the Japanese by Marshal Pétain's French colonial officials in Indochina and were backed by fighter jets.

Japanese infantry poured in from Thailand to capture airports in Kedah and Kelantan. Kuala Lumpur fell on 11 January 1942 and, five weeks later, Singapore was captured.

If Japanese treatment of Allied prisoners of war in Malaya was notoriously brutal, the attitude towards Asian civilians was more ambivalent. At first, the Japanese curtailed the privileges of the Malay rulers and forced them to pay homage to the Japanese Emperor. Then, to gain Malay support, the Japanese upheld their prestige, restored pensions and preserved their authority, at least in Malay customs and Islamic religion.

The Chinese were massacred. From 1943 Chinese communists led the resistance in the Malayan People's Anti-Japanese Army, aided by the British, to prepare for an Allied return.

The Emergency

The Japanese surrender left in place a 7,000-strong resistance army led by Chinese communists. Before disbanding, the army wrought revenge on Malays who had collaborated with the Japanese. This in turn sparked a brief wave of racial violence between Malays and Chinese.

To match their long-term stake in the country's prosperity, the Chinese and Indians wanted political equality with the Malays. Nationalists in the new United Malays National Organisation (UMNO) resented this 'foreign' intrusion imposed by 19th-century economic development. To

The National Monument in KL

give the Malays safeguards against economically dominant Chinese and Indians, the British created the new Federation of Malaya in 1948. Strong government under a High Commissioner left powers in the hands of the states' Malay rulers. Crown colony status was granted to Northern Borneo and Singapore, the latter excluded from the Federation because of its Chinese majority. The Chinese, considering their loyalty to the Allied cause in World War II, felt betrayed. Some turned to the Chinese-led Malayan Communist Party (MCP).

Four months after the creation of the Federation, three European rubber planters were murdered in Perak – the first victims in a guerrilla war launched by communist rebels. The British sent in troops, but the killing continued. The violence reached a climax in 1951, with the assassination of High Commissioner Henry Gurney.

Gurney's successor, General Gerald Templer, stepped in to deal with the 'Emergency'. He intensified military action, while cutting the political grass from under the communists' feet. Templer stepped up self-government, increased Chinese access to full citizenship and admitted those of Chinese origin for the first time to the Malayan Civil Service.

Under Cambridge-trained lawyer Tunku Abdul Rahman, brother of the Sultan of Kedah, UMNO's conservative Malays formed an alliance with the English-educated bourgeoisie of the Malayan Chinese and Malayan Indian Congress. During the Emergency, Chinese and Indian community leaders sought a solution. The Alliance won 51 of 52 seats in the 1955 election by promising a fair, multiracial constitution.

Independence

Independence or *merdeka* (freedom) came in 1957, and the Emergency ended three years later. The Alliance's English-educated elite imagined that multiracial integration would come about through education and employment. With a bicameral government under a constitutional monarchy, the Federation made Malay the compulsory language and Islam the official religion. Primary education could be in Chinese, Indian or English, but secondary education was in Malay.

Tunku Abdul Rahman, the first prime minister, reversed his party's anti-Chinese policy by offering Singapore a place in the Federation. With the defeat of Singapore's moderate Progressive Party by left-wing radicals, Tunku Abdul Rahman feared the creation of a communist state on his doorstep. As a counterweight to the Singapore Chinese, he brought in the North Borneo states of Sabah and Sarawak, granting them special privileges for their indigenous populations and funds to help to develop their economies.

To embrace the enlarged territory, the Federation took on the new name of Malaysia in September 1963, but Singapore, with its multiracial policies, sought to dismantle Malay privileges. Singapore's effort to reorganise political parties on a social and economic, rather than ethnic basis, misread Malay feelings. Riots broke out in 1964, and Tunku Abdul Rahman was forced to expel Singapore from the Federation.

Four days of racial riots in the federal capital in 1969 led to the suspension of the constitution and a state of emergency. The constitution was not restored until February 1971. The riots were a warning for the government, which was passing controversial legislation, such as the granting of special rights to Malays and the restriction of public gatherings.

Tun Abdul Razak became Prime Minister after the retirement of Tunku Abdul Rahman in 1970. Under his administration, emphasis was placed on improving the status of

The Prime Minister's palatial residence in Putrajaya

Malays and 'other indigenous peoples'. The government's aim was to broaden the distribution of wealth held by Malays.

On Tun Abdul Razak's death in 1976, Datuk Hussein Onn, a son of the founder of the UMNO, became prime minister, and UMNO became stronger just as Malaysian exports were growing. Combined political and economic strength set a sound base for Datuk Seri Dr Mahathir bin Mohamad (now Tun Mahathir), when he became Prime Minister in July 1981.

Under Dr Mahathir, Malaysia achieved remarkable economic prosperity. Rubber and tin declined in importance, but were supplemented by palm oil plantations, discoveries of petroleum and natural gas reserves off Borneo's north coast and the peninsula's east coast, and developments in manufacturing and tourism. Timber, which during the 1970s and 1980s brought valuable revenue, was reduced to conserve forests. In recent years, manufacturing, particularly electronics, represented a new direction away from a dependence on commodity exports.

The 21st Century

Malaysia entered the new millennium as a wealthy country with a sound economy. In October 2003, Datuk Seri Abdullah Ahmad Badawi took over the premiership, following Dr Mahathir's retirement. In the 2008 election, the coalition government received its biggest backlash in 50 years with the opposition winning the states of Kelantan, Selangor, Kedah, Penang and Perak. Voters expressed their concern over Badawi's leadership and his government's lack of direction.

On guard in Kuching

Historical Landmarks

c. 40,00BC Earliest known habitation at Niah Caves, Sarawak.

c. 2,500BC Proto-Malays spread south from Yunnan area in China.

AD500–1000 Development of Hindu-Buddhist trading kingdoms.

1303 Introduction of Islam to the Malay Peninsula.

c. 1400 Founding of Melaka by Srivijaya prince Parameswara.

1409 Chinese Admiral Cheng Ho arrives in Melaka.

1411 Parameswara converts to Islam and meets Ming Emperor of China.

1446 Melaka expands under Sultan Muzaffar Shah.

c. 1456–98 Prime Minister Tun Perak expands Melaka's empire.

1511 Melaka falls to the Portuguese.

1641 Dutch take Melaka from Portuguese.

1699–1784 Minangkabu-Bugis struggle for control of Strait of Malacca.

1786 British occupy Penang.

1824 Anglo-Dutch Treaty carves up Malay world into colonial spheres.

1841 James Brooke established as Rajah of Sarawak.

1875–6 Perak War and murder of the British Resident, James Birch.

1896 Federated Malay States (fms) are created.

1920–41 Early signs of Malay nationalism surface.

1941–5 Japanese conquest and occupation.

1945 British reoccupy Malaysia.

1948 Federation of Malaya inaugurated.

1948–60 Communist uprising – the so-called 'Emergency'.

1955 First general elections in the peninsula; victory for Alliance coalition.

1957 Malaya becomes independent.

1963 Creation of Federation of Malaysia.

1965 Following rioting, Singapore expelled from Federation.

1981–late 2003 Prosperity under Prime Minister Dr Mahathir.

1998 Kuala Lumpur hosts Commonwealth Games.

2004 Abdullah Ahmed Badawi wins election. Tsunami hits Penang and Kedah.

2005 Yearly tourism arrivals into Malaysia reach 16 million.

2008 Government wins election but with reduced majority as the opposition takes five states.

WHERE TO GO

Setting your priorities in Malaysia before you set off is essential to making your trip both pleasant and satisfying. Happily, many destinations offer a key that active travellers will be searching for, such as exploring Malaysia's culture and history or engaging in a sport like scuba diving. Often there is an added bonus: a nearby forest or a beach-side resort.

Malaysia's well developed transport infrastructure – rail, road and air – also offers the chance to step away from rigid planning if you desire to stay an extra day by the beach or want to do some more extensive shopping. Caution is needed if you are not used to a hot and humid climate and often requires a little extra planning when heading out on tour, trekking or just lazing by the pool.

Planning the Journey

The towns hold a mirror to Malaysia's ethnic blend of Malay, Chinese, Indians and Eurasians, living side by side or in their separate neighbourhoods. The northeast coast of Malaysia, especially between Kota Bharu and Kuantan, is one of the best places to see traditional Malay life with its rich Muslim culture, particularly evident in the *kampungs* (villages) of the interior. Step back into Malaysia's history in the port towns of Melaka or Kuala Terengganu, where colonial rivals once battled for supremacy, and where sultans controlled their sultanates. Your attention will also be captured by the beauty of the many mosques, temples, churches and shrines as the country's faithful practise their beliefs. In Melaka, observe the way of life of the Nyonyas and Babas, the oldest Chinese community, and its more modern manifestation in Penang.

Sunset on the peninsula's scenic east coast

Beyond urban limits you will find many opportunities to enjoy rural and forested Malaysia. But finding your way around the various rainforests, coral reefs or marine reserves can be bewildering if you plunge in unprepared. Unless you already have some experience in the region, use the services of one of the many first-class local tour operators *(see page 162)*.

Malaysia has done a fine job of providing visitors with access to its natural assets without 'taming' these resources too much. At the heart of the peninsula, the huge Taman Negara gives you the most comprehensive view of rainforest animals and plants in their natural state. A more 'compact' approach is possible on the islands, such as Tioman or Langkawi.

On the island of Borneo, the great natural attractions are Sarawak's caves at Niah and Mulu, river cruises with a visit to tribal longhouses, Sabah's national parks of Mount Kinabalu and the offshore islands, and the Sepilok Orang-utan

Beautiful Emerald Bay Beach on Pangkor Laut Island, Perak

Sanctuary. If your main desire is to escape the coastal heat, highland retreats will refresh and invigorate, by offering a chance to enjoy what was once the exclusive domain of colonial administrators.

White sandy beaches and gentle sea breezes are for many the perfect recipe for a holiday from the stresses of modern life, and in Malaysia the offerings are plentiful. Whether on the peninsula or in the marine parks of Sabah and Sarawak, you'll find many opportunities to bask and laze under the tropical sun (remember to use sunscreen and drink plenty of water to avoid sunburn and dehydration).

On the west coast the best beaches are on the island resorts of Pangkor and Langkawi. Unspoiled stretches of sand can also be found on the east coast, from Pantai Cahaya Bulan, north of Kota Bharu, down to Beserah, north of Kuantan. Further south are the resorts of Tioman Island and Desaru. In East Malaysia, Kuching and Kota Kinabalu have fine resort hotels.

Public affection

Physical displays of affection, such as holding hands or kissing in public, are frowned upon. Do not offer your hand to be shaken unless the other person extends their hand first.

THE CENTRE

Malaysia's prosperity in recent decades is most evident in the central region of the peninsula, where signs of wealth abound, from the new international airport to KL's dramatic skyline, to members of the middle class driving Malaysian-made Proton sedans on six-lane highways. But even as new light-rail systems wind through KL, progress has not entirely buried the past under chrome and concrete. Still thriving are the old commercial areas that brought so much wealth to the city and country.

Beyond KL, the British colonial past – whose structures now more often stand in the shadow of KL's skyscrapers –

continues to echo through hill stations. Here, amid the cool breezes or gentle mists of the Cameron Highlands, the English palate for tea (on a plantation scale) and strawberries thrives. Retreats within easier reach of KL – the casino of the Genting Highlands or theme parks born out of former tin mines – draw families for holidays, along with parks, zoos and aquariums.

Commerce and industry line the way to the port of Klang on the coast, while Ipoh is Perak's state capital made rich on tin, and Kuala Kangsar is the leisurely, royal state capital. The vast Taman Negara, which translates simply as national park, is one of the world's best-preserved primary rainforests and is home to many unique tropical plants and animals.

Kuala Lumpur

 At times **Kuala Lumpur** appears to be a maze of pedestrian-unfriendly overpasses and expressways. But the city opens to

KL's impressive skyline

islands of almost forest-like tree-cover before descending again into lively markets surrounded by the buildings that rise above the city's busy streets. Visitors may initially be drawn to the 88-storey Petronas Twin Towers or Menara Kuala Lumpur (KL Tower), which are symbols of modern KL. But the more fascinating splendours of the past are at street level, where distinctive neo-Gothic styles are beautifully preserved.

Sultan Abdul Samad Building

As in many other Malaysian cities, the population is predominantly Chinese. The Chinese community is prominent in the business world. Chinatown itself remains a hive of activity, located not far from Little India and its pungent spice shops and ornate Hindu temples. Ethnic Malays are present in all levels of the government and civil service.

The Historic Centre

KL's main historic quarter lies near Jalan Sultan Hishamuddin, where, on the east side of the broad avenue, is the **Sultan Abdul Samad Building**. The crypto-Moorish Federal Secretariat, once the **Supreme Court** and **High Court**, was begun in 1894 (finished in 1897) and capped with three copper onion-shaped domes. One tops a 40m (120ft) high clock tower bearing a similarity to London's Big Ben.

Among the many impressive skyscrapers, one of the most striking is the 35-storey **Dayabumi Complex** (1970), southeast of Dataran Merdeka. The soaring white tower integrates traditional Islamic architectural themes – pointed arches, delicate open tracery – with otherwise modern design. Included in the southernmost end of the complex is the adjoining **Pejabat Pos Besar** (General Post Office).

On the western side of the boulevard is the **Dataran Merdeka** (Freedom Square), where in colonial days the sound of a cricket bat would have been heard: it was here that members of the mock-Tudor **Royal Selangor Club** (1884) took time off from the affairs of the Empire to play cricket. On the wide lawn, independence was greeted by cheers on 31 August 1957. The Anglican **St Mary's Cathedral** is found on the square's northern side. The oldest church in KL, it began life in 1887 as a wooden shack on Bukit Aman before being relocated here. The present building remains a centre of worship and spiritual life for the city's Anglicans.

KL's old Railway Station at night

British architect A.B. Hubbock designed the **Malaysian Railway** buildings, located south on Jalan Sultan Hishamuddin. The old station (completed in 1911 and renovated in 1986) resembles a sultan's palace and is more attractive than the sombre brown headquarters building opposite. A fine example of Moorish architecture, it reflects the Ottoman and Moghul glory of the 13th and 14th centuries. While it is still a stop on the suburban network, the city's main rail hub is now KL Sentral, situated southwest of here near Muzium Negara.

Hubbock also designed the **Masjid Jamek**. Since 1909 this building has marked the confluence of the Gombak and Klang Rivers, where tin miners loaded supplies to be sent up-river and unloaded their tin for shipment west to Port Klang, and where the city's roots were set down. It was designed in 1907 by Hubbock in an Indian Moghul style: three-pointed domes over the prayer hall, two minarets and balustrades above an arcade of cusped arches – the whole predominant-ly gleaming white, with pink terracotta brick.

Across the river going east from the Dayabumi Complex is the old **Pasar Seni** (Central Market), set in an attractive art deco building (1936) in pastel blue and pink with a bold, bright skylit roof. Clothes and arts and crafts have replaced the fish, meat and vegetables that used to be sold here.

Chinatown

Southeast from the Central Market lie the exotic offerings of **Chinatown**, within the boundaries of Jalan Sultan, Jalan Bandar (now known as Jalan Tun H.S. Lee), and especially along **Jalan Petaling**. Here you will discover Chinese apothe-caries who display their medicines in porcelain jars, a mul-titude of restaurants and stalls, fortune-tellers and pet shops.

At night, when Jalan Petaling is closed to traffic, the area re-ally comes alive. Pedlars sell replica watches, CDs and DVDs, clothing, jewellery and ornaments; the side streets are full of open-air restaurants offering barbecued meats, seafood, noo-dles, rice-pots and do-it-yourself 'steamboats' (see page 148).

Past the Jalan Tun H.S. Lee and Jalan Cheng Lock junc-tion is the **Sze Ya Temple**, founded by Yap Ay Loy, once a city leader. The largest temple is **Chan See Shu Yuen**, built in 1906 and dedicated to Chong Wah, a Sung Dynasty em-peror. It also marks Chinatown's southern boundary.

A multicultural city

An arresting display of colour comes soon after the Kwoong Siew Association Temple, in the form of the **Sri Mahamariamman Hindu Temple** on Jalan Bandar. It was built in the style of a south Indian *gopuram* (temple gatehouse-tower), covered with a riot of colourful statuary from the Hindu pantheon. First erected in 1873, it was shunted across to its present site to make way for the railway station in 1855, and it is from here the annual Thaipusam pilgrimage to Batu Caves *(see page 43)* commences.

North and east of the historic centre is KL's 'Golden Triangle', a modern office, entertainment and shopping district. Nearby are two of the city's tallest landmarks. The **Petronas Twin Towers** are located north of the triangle and part of the **Kuala Lumpur City Centre (KLCC)**. On the 41st and 42nd floors there is a sky bridge open to the public, and below there is a concert hall, upmarket shopping mall and the interactive science centre, Petrosains. For the city's best views visit **Menara Kuala Lumpur** (Telekom Tower) which opened in 1996 and rises to 421m (1,381ft). The non-stop lift takes 55 seconds from ground to the observatory, and offers spectacular views. For those wanting to eat on the move, there is the Seri Angkasa Revolving restaurant at the top.

Cultural and Historical Sights

To the west of the old railway station and within view is **Masjid Negara** (National Mosque), a modern complex covering over 5 hectares (13 acres). On Friday and other important religious days it can house 8,000 worshippers under the tent-like stone roof of its Grand Hall. Walls of open-stone work support a canopy of 18 folds fanning out in a circle. These symbolise the 13 states of Malaysia and five pillars of Islamic faith. The mosque includes ceremonial rooms, a library and a meeting hall, set around pools mirroring the blue stained glass of the Grand Hall and marble galleries. Above it all is a 73m (239ft) high minaret, with a balcony from which the *muezzin* calls to prayer.

The **Muzium Negara** (National Museum) stands on Jalan Damansara south of the Lake Gardens. Opened in 1963, the building blends modern and traditional Malay design. Two glass mosaic murals flanking the entrance depict cultural and historical themes. Five main galleries cover such subjects as history, national sports and natural history.

Shopping in Suria KLCC

Other museums include the nearby **Islamic Arts Museum Malaysia**, which showcases the art and culture of the Islamic world. The **National History Museum** on Jalan Raja south of the Dataran Merdeka, with exhibits dating back 520 million years (quartzite rock), as well as a 40,000-year-old *Homo sapiens* skull. On the campus of the University of Malaysia is the **Asian Art Museum**, with exhibits of regional sculptures and textiles.

Taman Tasik Perdana (KL Lake Gardens)

West of the Masjid Negara are the **Taman Tasik Perdana** (Lake Gardens), 91 hectares (225 acres) of parkland landscaped in 1888 under British Resident Frank Swettenham. A popular place for picnicking, jogging and resting beneath the trees, it features a boating lake and provides a lovely escape from rushed city life. There is also a butterfly farm, orchid garden, deer park and bird park, the latter home to thousands of birds. Within the gardens is a **Planetarium** and an IMAX theatre.

On a hill at the northern end of the park across a main road, the **Tugu Negara** (National Monument) commemorates Malaysia's unsettled history through the Emergency *(see page 25)*. The bronze sculpture was designed by Felix de Weldon. Also on the monument grounds is a **Cenotaph** to the British Commonwealth's dead of the two World Wars. West of the monument, outside the park, is **Parliament House**, which holds the sessions of the Senate and House of Representatives.

Away From the City Centre

To see the **tin magnates' mansions** that remain standing, take a taxi ride along Jalan Ampang some 10km (6 miles) north-west of town. A few of these grand 19th- and 20th-century residences survive, tucked away among the skyscrapers, with forest growth often invading their gardens.

One of the best preserved is the Dewan Tunku Abdul Rahman, built in 1935 by Chinese tin and rubber mogul Eu Tong Sen. Nowadays it is the **Malaysia Tourism Centre**, which provides travel advice,

Malaysia Tourism Centre

brochures, computer work-stations and banking.

Night markets remain popular with Malaysians for cheap products and excellent local food. They are ideal for soaking up local colour and atmosphere. One of the cheapest markets is at **Chow Kit**, where Batu Road crosses Jalang Dang Wangi. Another market catering to more traditional tastes is the **Kampung Bahru** (New Village), behind the Chow Kit area. This market is a *Pasar Minggu* (Sunday Market), but like many other similar markets, it begins late on Saturday afternoon and trades on into the early hours of Sunday morning.

The Blue Mosque in Shah Alam, the capital of Selangor

Day Trips from Kuala Lumpur

Around Kuala Lumpur is the state of **Selangor**, an area that grew rich on tin and today is Malaysia's wealthiest and most developed state. While the emphasis in this region is clearly on industry, information technology and administration, there are a number of sites well worth visiting.

Shah Alam

Constructed in the 1970s on former rubber plantation land, **Shah Alam** is Selangor's capital and one of the country's best-planned cities with large houses and broad, tree-lined boulevards. **Masjid Sultan Salahuddin Abdul Aziz Shah** is ◄

the state mosque and the city's standout landmark, also known as the Blue Mosque because of its distinctive blue dome, which is bigger than that of St Paul's Cathedral in London. The mosque is laid out in the style of the Great Mosque of Mecca, with a prayer hall that can accommodate 16,000 worshippers. When touring the interior of the mosque, ensure that you are appropriately dressed (remember to remove your footwear), and that it is not prayer time.

Theme Parks

Just beyond the city there are several theme parks built out of the remains of the pits created from tin mining. The **Mines Wonderland** has been built on what was the world's largest open-cast mining operation. South of Kuala Lumpur along Jalan Sungai Besi, it includes snow-making facilities for a feel of winter in the tropics. **Sunway Lagoon** in Bandar Sunway, located near suburban Subang Jaya, is known for its water attractions and rides and is great entertainment for children.

Thaipusam Festival in the Batu Caves

The Batu Caves are the focus of the great Thaipusam Festival celebrating Lord Murugan receiving a sacred spear with which to vanquish the sources of evil.

Every January or February (depending upon the moon) thousands of Hindus gather to do penitence for past sins. The most fervent of them punish themselves by having their tongues or cheeks pierced with skewers, and hooks inserted in their bodies. Some also carry a *kavadi* (a frame bearing peacock feathers and statuettes of deities). Some simply carry jars of milk, rose-water, coconut or sugar-cane juice. During Thaipusam, as many as 500,000 people will crowd around the Batu Caves.

For tourists, the climb in humid heat up 272 steps to the cave-shrine entrance may be penitence enough.

Batu Caves

The giant **Batu Caves** are a popular excursion 45 minutes' drive north of town just off the Ipoh Road. Set in limestone cliffs hidden in the forest, they were 'discovered' in 1878 by a group of explorers. The caves were a hideout for anti-Japanese, communist guerrillas during World War II. Now transformed into a Hindu shrine, they receive the most attention during the Thaipusam Festival celebrated in the early months of each year.

There are in fact dozens of impressive limestone caves attracting botanists and zoologists to study their unique flora and fauna, but only

The Batu Caves have become a Hindu shrine

three are accessible to the general public. At the top of a 272-step staircase is the **Cathedral Cave**, the most breathtaking of the three, with its architectural columns of lofty stalactites and stalagmites. At the foot of the hill, a bridge over a pond leads to the **Art Gallery Cave**, with displays of garish statues of Hindu deities, and the **Poet's Cave**, where verses of the ancient Tamil poet Thiruvalluvar are painted directly on stone tablets.

Templer Park

Further north (another 9km/6 miles along the Ipoh Road) from the Batu Caves is **Templer Park**, which offers an insight into a Malaysian rainforest to those with little time to venture into the major national parks and forested areas. Named after Britain's last High Commissioner, Sir Gerald Templer, the park was conceived in 1950 as a vast forest retreat for the public. Covering an area of 1,200 hectares (2,965 acres), the rainforest comes complete with waterfalls, rushing streams, lagoons for swimming and caves to explore in the Bukit Takun limestone cliffs. There are several forest trails, with the highest point being **Bukit Takun** 740m (2,428ft) on the western side of the river in the park's northern corner.

The Highlands

By the time Malaysia came under the British imperial control in the late 18th century, colonial officials had fully developed the grand institution of the hill station, where they could cool off from the hot and humid lowlands in the days before air-conditioning. These havens of relaxation have now become

Temple overlooking the Genting Highlands

resorts, set among golf courses, gardens and orchards in
the mountain ranges of the
peninsula's interior. Nowadays, Malaysian families are
lured to the highlands closest
to Kuala Lumpur – Genting
and Fraser's Hill – while the
Cameron Highlands is most
popular with foreign visitors.
These retreats offer a range

Forest exploration

The forests, especially those
in the Cameron Highlands,
were once strongholds for
the rebels during the
Communist Emergency, so
some caution is required
when venturing into them;
good maps are a must, and
a guide is recommended
for most trails.

of leisure activities, including jungle trekking, horse riding
and golf, depending on the location.

Genting Highlands

Nearest of the highland resort areas to Kuala Lumpur at 51km
(32 miles), the **Genting Highlands** rise to 2,000m (6,560ft)
and are a far cry from the misty, forested mountains they once
were. Nowadays, descriptions of the resort and hotel complex
vary from big and bold to a 'one-stop destination for fantasy,
excitement and adventure'. You'll find a wide range of facilities, including an 18-hole golf course and theme parks with
cinemas, boat-rides, restaurants and ten-pin bowling. The resort's casino is Malaysia's only such legal gambling house.

Fraser's Hill

In contrast to the Genting Highlands, this charming, old-
fashioned hill station, located 100km (60 miles) northwest of
KL, is built across seven hills, its highest point being 1,500m
(4,920ft) in the Titiwangsa Range. These days it offers a cool
and peaceful retreat. The resort was named after Louis James
Fraser, an English adventurer and scoundrel, who dealt in
mule hides, tin, opium and gambling. Fraser had disappeared
mysteriously before the hill station came into being in 1910.

Road access may be difficult as landslides are common. The last 8km (5 miles) is a narrow road where an alternating, one-way traffic system operates. It was along this portion of road, marked by a signpost that reads 'Emergency Historical Site', where British High Commissioner Sir Henry Gurney was killed during the communist insurgency in 1951.

The countryside is wilder and less cultivated than that in the Cameron Highlands, but the sedate side of colonial life is also more recognisable here in the white-and-grey stone bungalows with lovely flowers in the gardens. You'll find a range of accommodation on offer, from Fraser's Pine and Silverpark Resorts in the top tier to more middle-range inns, bungalows and even a youth hostel. There are good tennis courts, a nine-hole golf course, playgrounds and horse riding.

Several nature trails are marked out through the nearby forests, and the wealth of birdlife means that forest walks are particularly enjoyable. Birdwatchers should look out for more than 270 species of birds, which may be seen in the immediate area. Montane species like cutia, although a Himalayan bird, are found here. Eagles are easy to spot soaring above the trees.

Alfred Russel Wallace, Nature Sleuth

A contemporary of Charles Darwin, Alfred Russel Wallace proved a true detective in his pioneering research in evolution theory and 'biogeography' – the geographical distribution of animals and plants. In Malaysia, he is best known as the 'discoverer' of the national butterfly, the green-and-black 'Rajah Brooke Birdwing'. But his most intriguing contributions came in the field of natural mimicry. Beyond the familiar camouflage techniques of chameleons and stick-insects, he watched viceroy butterflies trick birds by cultivating a resemblance to the monarch butterfly, which the birds hate. He also discovered ant-eating spiders that look like their prey.

Cameron Highlands

The finest of the cool hill resorts, 240km (150 miles) from KL, stands on a splendid plateau in rolling green valleys, surrounded by the rugged peaks of the Titiwangsa Range, the tallest of which is Mount Brinchang at 2,032m (6,664ft). If you've been travelling on the coast, or elsewhere in semitropical Southeast Asia, the **Cameron Highlands**, locat-

Many rare butterfly species are found in the Cameron Highlands

ed over 1,520m (4,987ft) above sea level, offer great relief amid morning mists and cool breezes.

Spread over three districts are the townships of **Ringlet**, Tanah Rata (the main township) and **Brinchang**. Ringlet township, the first point of arrival, offers very little that is special, apart from flower nurseries and access to some tea plantations. Continue 13km (7 miles) from Ringlet to reach Tanah Rata. On the road from Ringlet is the **Sultan Abu Bakar Lake**, formed by the damming of the Bertam River. Brinchang, just a few kilometres beyond Tanah Rata, is known for its farms, flower nurseries, fruit gardens and tea plantations.

The hill station was named after William Cameron, a British surveyor, who in 1885 reported the finding of the 'fine plateau'. He was soon followed by tea planters and Chinese vegetable growers. The Highlands also still hold the answer to the mysterious disappearance of wealthy American Thai-silk entrepreneur Jim Thompson, who went missing one evening in 1967 after setting off for a stroll while on holiday at the hill station.

For those using public transport, the Highlands can be reached by train on the KL–Butterworth line to Tapah Road

Station and then to the hills by taxi. The scenery changes from bamboo and palms to a denser rainforest of lush greenery, and then, as the temperature drops and the more comfortable mountain air takes over, montane oaks and laurels common in temperate climates. A new road from Simpang Pulai near Ipoh is less circuitous than the old road.

Tanah Rata has hotels, good Chinese and Indian restaurants, and English-style tearooms serving the local Cameronian brew together with cakes and locally grown strawberries with cream.

The main tea plantations are the **Boh**, **Blue Valley** and **Sungei Palas Tea Estates**. The latter features a **Tea Centre** (Tue–Sun), where you can learn about tea manufacturing, and sample various blends while enjoying great views of the estate.

Accommodation options in Tanah Rata vary depending on your budget, from international-class resorts, such as the Cameron Highlands Resort and The Lakehouse, to moderately

Extensive tea plantation in the Cameron Highlands

priced guesthouses. Worth a visit, even if you can't afford a room, is the **Smokehouse Hotel** near the golf course. The mock-Tudor resort has become an institution since it was built in the 1930s. An afternoon traditional 'cream tea' or English roast dinner is an experience in itself. Nearby is a fine 18-hole public golf course, beautifully landscaped and an enjoyable course to play because of the cool air.

The cooler climate makes forest walks here a special pleasure, not least of all for the many brightly coloured butterflies along the way, with almost a dozen officially listed. Two relatively well-marked paths from Tanah Rata, which are easy enough for the whole family, lead to swimming and picnic spots at **Parit Falls** and **Robinson Falls**. Other more challenging choices, for which you should enlist the help of a guide, take you up to **Mount Jasar** (1,696m/5,564ft) and **Mount Beremban** (1,841m/6,040ft). Besides the butterflies, look out for red-bellied squirrels, wild pigs and the occasional tapir. The best buys in the Camerons are fresh flowers, fruit and vegetables.

Perak

A journey to Perak takes travellers into what once was the key region for Malaysia's economic prosperity, standing as a lure to powerful states and interests as well as (mostly Chinese) migrant workers. Tin, the basis for the state's wealth, was once taken from diggings that claimed to be the largest such mines in the world. The wealth from the mines paid for many of the historical structures evident throughout the state. Perak, which means silver in Malay, is Peninsular Malaysia's second largest state, reaching from Tanjung Malim in the south to the Thai border, covering some 21,000 sq km (8,108 sq miles). Its sultan's family is also the last to be able to trace its ancestry to the 16th-century sultans of Melaka.

The capital Ipoh may be considered the capital of the world's tin industry. It superseded Perak's other rich mining capital, Taiping (formerly known as Larut), in this role in 1937. Kuala Kangsar is the royal capital and has been home to Perak's sultans since the 15th century.

The journey north from KL either by train or car takes you through a captivating landscape of forests and plantations, reaching back from the coastal plains to climb the blue hills of the Titiwangsa Range. This wild beauty is enhanced by spectacular outcrops of limestone rock and various cave systems.

Ipoh

Once the harbour for all incoming junks and sampans from the Strait of Malacca (Selat Melaka) through the Perak River, the city of **Ipoh** is located on the Kinta River 220km (135 miles) north of KL. Ipoh offers good accommodation and amenities, including a range of restaurants with Chinese specialities, such as steamed chicken with bean sprouts and noodles.

Colonial influences are clearly evident in the **railway station**, whose Moghul architecture is reminiscent of KL's old station and is locally nicknamed 'the Taj Mahal'; inside is the Majestic Station Hotel. The **High Court** and **Hong Kong and Shanghai Bank** buildings are also excellent examples of architecture from the Edwardian era. Other memories of the British presence are in the **clock tower**, commemorating the first British resident of Perak, James Birch, who was assassinated in 1875. **St Michael's School** and the **Royal Ipoh Club** are also monuments of the colonial era.

Around Jalan Dato' Sagor and the nearby streets are some of the best-preserved examples of **Chinese architecture** in

Malaysia. For an insight into the local tin mining industry, visit the excellent **Geological Museum** on Jalan Sultan Azlan Shah. In addition to exhibits of Perak's rich variety of minerals, ores and fossils are models of tin mining equipment.

Outside the city, amid vast caves in limestone outcrops, are a number of Buddhist temples. In the south the **Sam Poh Tong Temples** are located within high limestone caves and cavities near **Gunung Rapat**. The latter dates back to 1890s, while the present facade was built in the 1950s, with the temple still home to a group of monks and nuns. Six kilometres (4 miles) north of Ipoh is the **Perak Tong**, built in 1926 by a Buddhist priest from China. Here the main attraction is a 13m (41ft) sitting Buddha within the darkened cavern; altogether there are more than 40 Buddha statues.

Saved from the over-growth of foliage in the past two decades, 12km (7 miles) from Ipoh is **Kellie's Castle**, a

Kellie's Castle was destined never to be finished

mansion whose construction was halted when its owner, William Kellie Smith, a rubber planter, died in Portugal in the mid-1920s. Further south, in **Teluk Intan**, is Malaysia's equivalent of the leaning tower of Pisa. The pagoda-like structure, built in 1885, is 25.5m (84ft) tall.

Kuala Kangsar

Home to the sultans of Perak for the past 500 years, **Kuala Kangsar** is built on a reach of the Perak River (Sungai Perak) 50km (32 miles) from Ipoh just off the highway. The town has two royal palaces; the brash stone residence **Istana Iskandariah**, and the more elegant traditional timbered **Istana Kenangan**, now used as a Royal Museum. The town is also where Malaysia's rubber industry started, with the planting of nine seedlings by former resident Hugh

The striking domes and minarets of the Ubadiah Mosque, one of the most photographed Islamic buildings in Malaysia

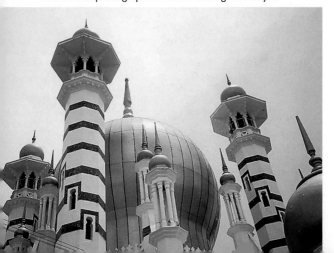

Low in 1877. One of the originals still survives near the district office on Jalan Raja Bendahara. The most striking building, set on a grass mound, is the **Ubadiah Mosque**, with its golden dome of glowing copper.

Kuala Kangsar has long been famous for the **Malay College**, set amid spacious grounds near the centre of town. This has been a prestigious and exclusive school for the education of the children of the Malay aristocracy since it was founded by the British in 1904. It is now open to the best scholars from all sections of Malay society.

Taiping

Another 30 minutes' drive from Kuala Kangsar, the old mining town of **Taiping** was formerly known as Larut. Its present-day name, meaning 'everlasting peace', was proposed by Britain as part of its diplomatic contribution to the end of the bloody feuds between Chinese secret societies fighting over control of the tin mining industry in the 1870s. They were forced to end their conflict under the Treaty of Pangkor in 1874, after British intervention.

Happily boasting the peninsula's heaviest rainfall, Taiping, the former capital of Perak state, is now a sleepy town full of large trees overhanging its wide streets. It has a magnificent 62-hectare (153-acre) park, **Lake Gardens**, landscaped from a tin mine abandoned in 1890. The grounds are now home to a 9-hole golf course, a small zoo, which offers a night safari tour, and an old **Government Rest House** (now a hotel).

Built in 1883, the **Perak Museum**, housing an interesting display of ancient weapons and Orang Asli implements, is the oldest in Malaysia. On the way, you will pass **Taiping Prison**, used by the Japanese in World War II and then for guerrilla troops captured during the Emergency.

Beyond the Lake Gardens, the **Taiping War Cemetery** bears impressive witness to the peninsula's early role in the

Pacific War against the Japanese. The tombs of soldiers of the Royal Australian Air Force, Indian Army Corps of Clerks, Ambulance Sepoy of the Indian Army Medical Corps and Royal Air Force reveal that many of them died on the very first day of active duty: 8 December 1941.

Once a tea estate, cool, cloud-enshrouded **Bukit Larut** (Maxwell Hill), 12km (7½ miles) northeast of Taiping, is Malaysia's smallest and oldest hill station. At 1,035m (3,400ft) above sea level, it has great views when the misty rain-clouds break. Near the jeep terminal, several bungalows and rest houses offer rooms for rent, but you must book in advance.

Night falls on Pangkor Laut

Pulau Pangkor

The largest of the nine islands lying offshore in the Strait of Malacca is **Pulau Pangkor**. Its beaches offer aquatic activities and there are nearby forest walks. The ferry from Lumut, about 50km (31 miles) south of Taiping, to Pangkor Island takes about 45 minutes. Once there, you'll find the wide sands of the **Pantai Puteri Dewi** (Beach of the Beautiful Princess) along the 122-hectare (301-acre) island's northern shore. An adjoining private island and one of the most exclusive destinations in Asia, **Pangkor Laut Resort** attracts well-heeled tourists.

Taman Negara

➤ **Taman Negara** national park provides an ideal setting for exploring vast rainforest, fast-flowing rivers and mountains of the peninsula's Main Range. It covers an area of 4,343 sq km (1,676 sq miles), spreading across three states: Pahang, Terengganu and Kelantan.

Backpackers may want to go it alone, but most people are advised to plan their visit through a tour operator. Armed with an entry permit, visitors head first to the park headquarters, 300km (187 miles) northeast of the national capital by road via Jerantut and 60km (37 miles) by motor-powered longboat from Kuala Tembeling.

The **boat ride** on the Tembeling River is likely to be one of the highlights of your visit. Along the way, you may see Orang Asli fishermen – the only human residents allowed by park authorities to stay here – setting their nets. Keep a look out, too, for water buffalo taking a bath, monitor lizards of sometimes over a metre in length, and even an occasional otter. Among the birds, you will see the flash of a kingfisher or hornbill. Wear a hat and bring along plenty of bottled water. The journey usually takes about three hours, even longer when short stretches of the river dry up, occasionally forcing passengers to walk along the riverbank while the boatmen push the sampan through the shallows.

The headquarters at **Kuala Tahan** have a good range of accommodation – chalets and bungalows in the Mutiara Resort – plus a restaurant and a general store. *(For trekking requirements, see page 162.)* The park headquarters organise informative evening slide-shows as a general introduction to the features of the rainforest.

Forest Trails

There are marked trails leading from the park's headquarters into the forest. Guides use them for organised walking and boat tours, but you can, of course, go off with your own group. There are both day trips and overnight tours to observation-hides, from where you can watch for wildlife visiting nearby salt-licks and watering holes. Overnight stays are organised at several observation-hides *(bumbun)*, namely at **Kumbang**, **Yong**, **Tabing**, **Belau** and **Cegar Anjing**. Park headquarters will provide sheets if you do not have a sleeping bag. The

River rapids make for a wild ride

most popular walk is across the elevated canopy trail, 20m (66ft) above the ground. From park headquarters, day trips leaving in the early morning include a walk to Bukit Indah, followed by a boat ride through the rapids to **Kuala Trenggan**, returning to headquarters on foot; a walk to the **Tabing Hide**, followed by a boat ride to the **Lata Berkoh** rapids, then another trek back to headquarters; a boat ride on the Tembeling River to the **Gua Telinga** (Bat Cave), which you enter on hands and knees until you can stand. You then find yourself in a great vault inhabited by hundreds of fruit- and insect-eating bats, which have little interest in humans. Only the squeamish will object to the giant toads and harmless little white cave-racer snakes.

The most adventurous trek for experienced walkers and climbers is a full nine-day walk up and down the peninsula's highest peak, **Mount Tahan** (2,187m/7,173ft) high. A jungle guide must accompany the group on the strenuous climb.

Flora and Fauna

The dipterocarp rainforest here includes the *tualang* tree. At 50m (164ft), it is the tallest tree in Southeast Asia. Among the exotic forest fruit are mango, durian, rambutan and various kinds of wild banana. At heights above 1,500m (5,000ft), you will see montane trees from the oak and laurel families.

With patience and luck by day, or rotating shift watches by night, you may see wild pigs, sambars, barking deer, gibbons, pig-tailed macaques, leaf monkeys, tree shrews or flying squirrels. Visitors to the Kumbang Hide have sometimes even caught sight of rare tigers and leopards.

During the fruit season, birdwatchers have spotted up to 70 species just around the park headquarters. Among them are lesser fish eagles, crested serpent eagles, fire-back pheasants and garnet pittas. From September to March you can also see migrant Arctic warblers, Japanese paradise flycatchers and Siberian blue robins.

Even if you do not spot much of the wildlife mentioned here – and you are bound to see something – the sheer experience of the forest at night, with its incredible noises, the flitting of mysterious fireflies and the sense of invisible but omnipresent life and movement around you will make it all worthwhile.

Taman Negara's frog life

THE WEST COAST

For the romantics, the township names of Port Dickson and Melaka (also known as Malacca) on the west coast evoke stories of the glorious past of sailing ships and Chinese junks carrying spices, silks and gold, of pirates and cutlasses and of noble men and beautiful princesses. In many ways, this is the story of Malaysia's southwest coastline. Nowadays, the rich tapestry of history lies in the monuments and old homes as well as the descendants of the colonisers – Malay and Indian, Chinese, Portuguese, Dutch and British. In the far north, Penang is both a holiday destination and a commercial centre, while closer to the border with Thailand, Langkawi Island is a leading resort for those in search of white sands, gentle seas, a scenic landscape and duty-free goods.

Melaka, Malaysia's first major city, is a patchwork quilt of architectural styles and international influences

South from Kuala Lumpur to Melaka

The highway from Kuala Lumpur and Selangor leads through Negeri Sembilan, the 'nine states' federated as one in the 18th century. You travel past vast palm oil and rubber plantations to the state capital of Seremban, 64km (40 miles) southwest of Kuala Lumpur.

Seremban

Here, the distinctive Min-angkabau buffalo-horn roofs of Sumatran (Indonesian) heritage are evident, togeth-er with the more recent colonial Victorian style and the tra-ditions of Chinese commercial shophouses. The main attractions are the **State Legislative Assembly Building**, a nest of nine roofs, one for each founding state; and the **Taman Seni Budaya Negeri** (Arts and Culture Complex). Visit the state museum located within the complex, where weapons as well as brass and silverware and a tableau por-traying a grand royal wedding are on display. In the grounds opposite is the Kampung Ampang Tinggi, a Malay prince's residence built entirely of wood. The neoclassical **State Library**, with its imposing colonial facade, was once the State Secretarial Building. Situated opposite are the exten-sive **Lake Gardens**.

> **He who is greatest**
>
> Negeri Sembilan's ruler is not a sultan but a Yam Tuan Besar or Yang Di Pertuan Besar, meaning 'He Who is Greatest'.

Sri Menanti

For what is probably the best original example of Minang-kabau architecture, take a side trip to the old royal capital, 37km (23 miles) east of Seremban on the Kuala Pilah Road. The ruler's palace, **Istana Lama**, was the official residence of the state royal family until 1931, replacing an earlier palace which had burnt down. The palace features 99 pil-lars, denoting 99 warriors of various *luak* (clans).

Melaka

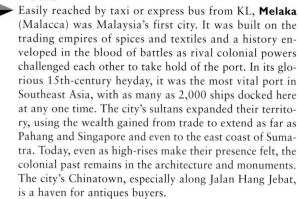

Easily reached by taxi or express bus from KL, **Melaka** (Malacca) was Malaysia's first city. It was built on the trading empires of spices and textiles and a history enveloped in the blood of battles as rival colonial powers challenged each other to take hold of the port. In its glorious 15th-century heyday, it was the most vital port in Southeast Asia, with as many as 2,000 ships docked here at any one time. The city's sultans expanded their territory, using the wealth gained from trade to extend as far as Pahang and Singapore and even to the east coast of Sumatra. Today, even as high-rises make their presence felt, the colonial past remains in the architecture and monuments. The city's Chinatown, especially along Jalan Hang Jebat, is a haven for antiques buyers.

The Old Centre

The main buildings of historical or cultural significance are all within easy walking distance of the old centre, Dutch Square, down by the Melaka River.

The square is situated just off **Melaka Bridge**. Spanning the river, the bridge was once the town's main strategic link between the port and city and the site of major battles against the European invaders.

The most prominent building overlooking the square is the Dutch **Stadthuys** (Town Hall), dating from around 1650. It was originally the official residence of Dutch governors and their officers. Behind the red facade is a structure built of masonry hauled from the Portuguese citadel. Since 1980 the building has housed the Museum of Ethnography and History, tracing the town's colonial and Malay past.

In the middle of the square is the **Queen Victoria Jubilee Fountain**, flanked by a mouse-deer statue.

Christ Church, with an imposing red exterior, was built between 1741 and 1753, in commemoration of the centenary of the Dutch occupation. Additions to the church were made by the British in the 19th century. Each of the long ceiling beams of the interior is hewn from one tree.

The archway and gate of the **A Famosa** fortress is all that remains of the 16th-century Portuguese fort next to the Stadthuys. It was saved from total destruction by Sir Stamford Raffles, then a government secretary in Penang. The date, 1670, and coat of arms were added to the gateway by the Dutch East India Company. The gate steps lead to the remains of **St Paul's Church**, built by a Portuguese captain, Duarte Coelho, as a chapel in 1521. Originally known as the Church of Our Lady of the Annunciation, it was re-named by the Dutch, who captured Melaka in 1641, and fell into disuse when Christ Church was built. In front of the church tower is a **statue of St Francis Xavier**, the Spanish Jesuit missionary who visited Melaka several times from 1545 until his death in 1553. In the church, a stone slab marks his tomb, empty since his remains were transported to Goa in India. Granite tombstones from the Dutch era stand against the walls. A Dutch and British **cemetery** is to be found further down the hill.

Melaka's Christ Church

The **Tugu Pengistiharn Kemerdekaan** (Proclamation of Independence Memorial) occupies a villa built in 1912, which was once the Malacca Club for British colonials and local planters. It was on the club's *padang* (playing field) that the nation's first Prime Minister Tunku Abdul Rahman announced in 1956 the success of his London negotiations. Nowadays, the memorial building shows films and displays documents tracing the campaign for independence. Several old hotels in town are located in historic buildings and their guests can learn much about the architecture of these grand homes.

Back towards the river is one of Melaka's more recent additions, the **Maritime Museum**, housed in a model of the *Flor De La Mar*, a Portuguese ship laden with bullion and other valuables that sank off Melaka. Exhibits include models of ships that have called at the port over its long history.

The Proclamation of Independence Memorial is housed in a former colonial clubhouse

The **Istana Kesultanan Melayu** (Malay Sultanate Palace) is a cultural museum standing amid elegant gardens north of the Porta de Santiago. Reconstructed from ancient prints, it is an approximate but noteworthy replica of Mansur Shah's grandiose hilltop residence, which is believed to have burned down in 1460.

Malay Sultanate Palace

Chinatown

The living history of Melaka is to be found among the Baba Nyonya community; the descendants of the original Chinese pioneers and entrepreneurs who married local Malay women in the old Straits Settlements of Melaka, Penang and Singapore.

The narrow streets of Melaka's **Chinatown**, just next to the river, resound with the past, especially the 19th century, when entrepreneurs from this community helped lift the local economy. Their contribution now stands among the houses along **Jalan Tun Tan Cheng Lock**, also known as 'Millionaires' Row'. This is a paradise for antiques hunters, filled with new and old Oriental treasures – porcelain, statues, jewellery, silverware and ornate 19th-century furniture. Head to Jalan Hang Jebat (formerly Jonker Street) for more browsing and bargain hunting.

One of these mansions, at 50 Jalan Tun Tan Cheng Lock, is the **Baba Nyonya Heritage Museum**, an amalgam of three houses belonging to one family. Built in 1896 by rubber planter Chan Cheng Siew, this house offers a vivid insight into the life and culture of the Straits Chinese, as the Babas are also known. In a style best described as Chinese Palladian, with its neoclassical columns and heavy hardwood doors, the

Baba Nyonya culture blends
Chinese and Malay traditions

furnishings and decor bear witness to the great prosperity of Baba entrepreneurs. A member of the Chan family usually gives guided tours of the house, which last about 45 minutes, and will point out its finer points – the silks, filigree, silver ornaments, gleaming blackwood furniture inlaid with ivory or mother-of-pearl, and a monumental gilded teak staircase leading to the bedrooms on the upper floor.

Along Jalan Tokong and Jalan Tukang Emas are Chinese and Hindu temples and a Muslim mosque. The **Cheng Hoon Teng Temple** (Evergreen Cloud Temple), originally built in 1646 by 'Kapitan China' Lee Wei King, a fugitive from China, claims to be Malaysia's oldest Chinese temple. Dedicated to Kuan Yin, it is flamboyantly decorated with multicoloured birds and flowers made from glass and porcelain. The bronze statue of Kwan Yin, the Goddess of Mercy, was brought back from India in the 19th century. The **Kampung Kling Mosque**, on Jalan Tokong (1748), has a multi-tiered roof with a watchtower-style minaret. The nearby **Sri Poyyatha Vinayagar Moorthi Temple** (1781), dedicated to the elephant god Ganesh, or Vinayagar, is also one of the oldest in the country. On Jalan Kampung Pantai is the **Mausoleum of Hang Jebat**, a 16th-century warrior who was killed unjustly in a duel of honour with his friend Hang Tuah, who has a water well named after him at Kampung Duyong.

Outside the City Centre

Rather than drive around the sights away from the old city centre, you may prefer to let a trishaw-driver find the way. Start perhaps with an evening ride past the open-air restaurants on Jalan Taman, better known as **Glutton's Corner**. Until the recent land reclamation for new housing developments, these Malay, Chinese and Tamil Indian eating places bordered the seafront, but the cuisine (the most notable dish being the spicy *mee hoon* noodles) has not changed.

Baba Nyonya

The Baba Nyonya community of Melaka (*baba*, male, *nyonya*, female) demonstrates the Chinese genius for adapting to local circumstances without losing the essentials of their own culture. Their subtle blend of Chinese and Malay traditions began back in the 15th century, when the entourage of Princess Hang Li Po, daughter of the Emperor of China and betrothed to Mansur Shah of Melaka, intermarried with local gentry. Their numbers were boosted in subsequent centuries by the influx of merchants and entrepreneurs, largely from Fukien in southern China.

The Chinese talent for business made a cheerful union with the Malay taste for pleasure, culminating in the joyously ostentatious affluence of the 19th and early 20th centuries. The Babas made their money from spices, rubber, timber and tin, and got their pleasure from gambling, chewing on betel nut, or an occasional pipe of opium. Their Nyonyas happily spent the family fortune on opulently furnished houses and in preparing elaborate trousseaus for their daughters.

Baba Nyonya cuisine is a triumphant synthesis of southern Chinese delicacies and the spice and pungency of Tamil-influenced Malay ingredients – garlic, red-hot chilli and rich coconut milk.

Bukit Cina

Inland, the hillside provides a Chinese cemetery for more than 12,000 graves, mostly horseshoe-shaped tombs. On the hilltop you will see the foundations of the 16th-century Portuguese Franciscan monastery and get a splendid view of the town and the Strait of Malacca. The gaudy **Sam Po Kong Temple** stands at the foot of Bukit Cina, honouring Cheng Ho, the eunuch admiral who in 1409 opened up Melaka to Chinese trade. Nearby is the **Perigi Raja** (Sultan's Well), dug in the 15th century.

➤ The Portuguese Settlement

A short drive some 3km (2 miles) south of the town centre along Jalan Parameswara takes you to the heart of this little Eurasian community, peopled by descendants of the Portuguese colonists. In the area around Jalan d'Albuquerque and **Dataran Portugis** (Portuguese Square), the houses look no

Some Portuguese descendants still speak the old *Cristao* dialect

different from those in the rest of Melaka, but you may hear snatches of *Cristao*, a 16th-century Portuguese dialect. The restaurants on and off the square serve good seafood, though over the centuries the Portuguese cuisine has taken on a spicy Asian flavour. The community worships at the simple,

Do not touch

Touching people on the head is considered rude, as the head is thought to be the most noble part of the body. Also, do not show anyone the soles of your feet, which are, conversely, the least dignified part of the body.

unassuming **St Peter's Catholic Church**, where Easter is an especially big event, attracting many Indians, Chinese and Malay non-Catholics to the great, candlelit procession.

The Coast Roads

It is worth taking a ride north along the Jalan Tengkera coast road to visit some of the picturesque fishing villages. On the way, take a look at the fine three-tiered, Sumatra-style **Tranquerah Mosque** (1748), the burial place of Sultan Hussain Shah of Johor, who negotiated with Raffles the British rights to Singapore. You will find good crab and shrimp at the fishing village of **Pantai Kundor**. Further north, **Tanjung Bidara**, 35km (20 miles) from Melaka, has a hotel resort and some pleasant shade trees on the beach for picnics.

Some 8km (5 miles) south of Melaka, you can take a boat at Umbai out to **Pulau Besar**, which has white sandy beaches and a forest offering pleasant walks.

Penang

On the northeast coast of **Penang** (Pulau Pinang, meaning Betel Nut Island), George Town is the island's main attraction, with rich colonial and historic roots amid the clutter of a market and commercial town. (The city is often referred to simply as

Taking a ride in George Town

'Penang'.) Its narrow streets and busy thoroughfares add to the adventure, with its Chinese history reflected in the shophouses and old hotels. Entry points to the island are by road and rail, a ferry journey across the Selat Selatan from the industrial town of Butterworth, or by way of the 7km (4½-mile) drive over the Penang Bridge, which provides wonderful views of the harbour. Flights, including international arrivals, land at the Bayan Lepas International Airport, which is some 18km (11 miles) south of George Town.

Most of Penang's activity is in the city, but it is also possible to relax at a beach-side resort or to flee the heat by taking the funicular railway link to the top of Penang Hill. You can step back into the island's history amid the colonial buildings, Chinese temples and shophouses. Delicious food and great shopping add to Penang's charm.

Under the British, Penang was named Prince of Wales Island, and the capital took its name from the son of King George III. Nowadays, Penang has the second largest economy among the states of Malaysia, with a population of over one million. It is also the centre for the country's electronics industry. The tsunami of Boxing Day 2004 swept a number of victims from the island's coast, although the damage wrought was considerably less than in other affected countries.

George Town

Today, **George Town** is a striking blend of historic structures and tall modern buildings. Move from the rich, scented air surrounding the Chinese temples to such modern buildings as the 65-storey **Komtar** – or Tun Abdul Razak Complex – a centre for government offices, shopping and entertainment.

Old Centre

One of the joys of touring George Town's historic section is the opportunity to cover many of the sites in this compact area by foot, and the best place to begin your tour is the main ferry terminal at **Weld Quay**. Along the foreshore there is the Kampung Ayer, or Chinese Water Village, better known as the **Clan Piers**, a hamlet of houses on stilts, joined by wooden walkways over the water and inhabited by 2,000 boatmen and fishing families, each group belonging to a different clan.

At the other end of Pengkalan Weld, opposite the Tourist Office, is the **Jam Besar** (Penang Clock Tower), presented to the town in 1897 to mark Queen Victoria's Diamond Jubilee.

Across the road is **Fort Cornwallis** (named after Charles Cornwallis, Governor General of India), which marks the spot where Captain Light arrived on 17 July 1786. The greenery of the park and gardens surrounds the fortifications, which were originally made of wood and rebuilt in 1810. **Jln Tun Syed Sheh Barakhbah** (also known as the Esplanade) runs between the waterfront and the Padang before the fort. This area is lined with handsome, 19th-century colonial government

Penang Clock Tower

buildings and their brilliant white is highly evocative of the era in which they were built. The British worshipped in **St George's Church** (1818) on Lebuh Farquhar. It is the oldest Anglican church in Southeast Asia. In the nearby cemetery, set among frangipani trees, is the **grave of Francis Light**, who died from malaria in 1794, only eight years after the start of his Penang adventure. The tombstones of many other graves reveal the hardships of the town's history.

Francis Light's statue stands at the entrance of the **Penang Museum** at the corner of Lebuh Light and Lebuh Farquhar. In fact, as no photograph of Light existed, the sculpture is a likeness made from a portrait of his son, William (who founded the city of Adelaide in South Australia). The museum is housed in what was the Penang Free School. Founded in 1816, it was the first English-language school in Southeast Asia. There is a fine collection of historical memorabilia, old paintings, etchings and a 19th-century Chinese bridal chamber. Also on show is one incongruous exhibit left by the Royal Air Force: a bronze bust of the German Kaiser Wilhelm II. The Penang Gallery at the Dewan Sri Pinang in Lebuh Light displays batik paintings, oils, graphics and Chinese ink drawings.

One of the great monuments from George Town's colonial days is the **Eastern & Oriental Hotel** at 10–12 Lebuh Farquhar. Even if you are not staying in one of the hotel's grand

Light in the Forest

On the northeast corner of the waterfront, Kedah Point marks the spot where the Penang settlement's founder Francis Light (see page 19) is said to have hit upon a cunning method of getting the surrounding forest cleared to make way for the town. He loaded a cannon with Spanish silver dollars, fired them into the forest, and invited local labourers to hack their way through the undergrowth to get to the money.

old rooms – where Rudyard Kipling and Somerset Maugham both stayed – take a drink in the venerable Farquhar's Bar, overlooking the harbour which is always lined with vessels from around the world. The E & O is actually a fusion of two separate hotels: the Eastern, facing the Esplanade, and the Oriental, facing the sea. It was the brainchild of Martin and Tigran Sharkie, Armenian brothers who also created the famous Raffles Hotel in Singapore. Restored to its former splendour, it is now one of a select group of heritage hotels in Southeast Asia.

Francis Light, founder of Penang

Chinatown

The heartland of George Town's **Chinatown** is centred on **Lebuh Chulia** and **Lebuh Campbell**, both of which run off the city's main commercial thoroughfare of Jalan Penang. Here, amid a sea of shophouses and busy streets, wares spill out, competing for space and the attention of shoppers. It is also an area favoured by backpackers, lured by cheap hotels and restaurants and its central location near historic sights. You will be able to find good leather and canvas-wear for forest treks on Campbell and Chulia streets. Here also are the betting shops, ancient barber shops and stores offering exotic medicines.

Wander around the neighbourhood's back streets to admire the well-maintained residential houses, many with elegantly carved teak window screens and doorways and handsome gold-and-black lacquered name plates. The more flamboyant are the **Clan Houses**, bulwarks of community solidarity. They combine temples for ancestral worship with meeting halls to settle local problems – housing, jobs, medical care, help for orphans and discreetly handled intra-community crime.

Off Lebuh Cannon – so called because of the holes made in the road surface here by cannonballs fired during the Great Penang Riot of 1867 – and through a laneway is the **Khoo Kongsi** (clan house of the family Khoo). Approach it via a narrow alley near the intersection of Jalan Acheh and Lebuh Pitt. Inside is an image of the clan's patron, Tua Sai Yeah, a renowned general of the Ch'in dynasty (221–207BC). Other houses nearby date back to the mid-19th century. The ornate ancestral temple **Leong San Tong** stands opposite a smaller hall used for open-air Chinese opera and theatre. To the left is a shrine to the God of Prosperity and to the right is the hall of *sinchoo* (soul-tablets), gold plaques honouring clan dignitaries and simpler wooden panels for more humble clan members.

The **Cheong Fatt Tze Mansion** on Lebuh Leith, built around 1860 by Thio Thaw Siat, a Chinese businessman, is considered one of the best examples of 19th-century Chinese architecture in Penang. Restored to its former glory, this 38-room, five-courtyard house gained Unesco recognition in 2000 and is now a boutique hotel. Tours are conducted twice a day for a small fee.

Clan associations

Chinese immigrants arriving in Malaysia in the 19th century fell under the protection and control of clan associations, similar in function to medieval European guilds.

The busiest public temple in Penang is the **Kuan Yin Teng Temple**, on Lebuh Pitt (Jalan Masjid Kapitan Kling), near St George's Church. Dedicated to the Goddess of Mercy, who has benevolent powers and is identified with the Indian Boddhisattva of Fertility, it draws both the rich and poor to pay respect and is popular with newly-wed couples. The atmosphere is heavy with the scent of burning joss-sticks mixed with the aroma of flowers, scented oils, fruits, cakes and roast chicken, offered on the altars to help solve family problems.

On the same street is the **Kapitan Kling Mosque**, the state's oldest mosque, built in 1800 for Muslim Indian soldiers. The **Sri Mariamman Temple** on Lebuh Queen (which runs parallel to Lebuh Pitt) was built in 1883 and is the oldest Hindu temple in Penang. Vividly decorated, it is dedicated to Lord Subramaniam, the son of Shiva and destroyer of evil, who is the focus of worship during the Thaipusam festival held in the early months of the year.

The Khoo Kongsi

Beyond the City Centre

The famous **flea market** is now located at **Lorong Kulit** (literally Skin Lane), near the city's stadium. Here you can wade through mountains of old clothes, jewellery, household utensils, clocks, dolls, ornaments, old coins and all the bric-a-brac of an Oriental bazaar.

The other main sights of interest outside downtown George Town are Penang Hill and the Botanical Gardens. The drive out along **Jalan Sultan Ahmad Shah** takes you

Kek Lok Si Temple

past the rubber magnates' huge neo-Gothic and Palladian mansions, built during the boom that lasted through World War I.

The Buddhist **Wat Chayamangkalaram monastery**, on Lorong Burma, is famous for its 33m (108ft) long reclining Buddha. The site for the temple was given to the community by Queen Victoria in 1845. The gigantic *naga* serpents, mystical creatures linking earth to heaven, are the balustrades at the entrance to the meditation hall.

Further west, away from the temple, you'll find the **Botanical Gardens**. The 30-hectare (74-acre) garden was created in 1844 as a tribute to Charles Curtis, its superintendent, who collected botanical specimens from the nearby hills. Leaf monkeys and long-tailed macaques are among the wildlife.

Jalan Dato Keramat, then Jalan Air Itam, lead west from the town to **Penang Hill**, 830m (2,722ft) above sea level, which served as a colonial hill station in the early 20th century. Take a slow ride on the funicular railway (built in 1923) past bungalows and villas set amid tropical gardens for panoramic views of the island. Birdwatchers should look out for blue-tailed bee-eaters, sunbirds and spider-hunters.

Above the small town of Air Itam stands the **Kek Lok Si** (Temple of Paradise). It was founded by Abbot Beow Lean, a Chinese Buddhist priest from Fujian Province in China who arrived in Penang in 1887. The temple's construction began in 1890 and took 20 years to complete. The centrepiece is the seven-tiered **Pagoda of a Million Buddhas**, which is 30m (98ft) high and dedicated to Tsi Tsuang Wang. The pagoda is actually a blend of three architectural styles, a Chinese octagonal base, a Thai central core and a Burmese peak. Inside the shrine are statues of the Laughing Buddha, radiating happiness; Sakyamuni Buddha, incarnation of the faith's founder; and Kuan Yin, the Goddess of Mercy.

Around The Island

Away from George Town's hectic, bustling streets and midday heat, there is the chance to explore the remainder of the island. A tour around the island – about 74km (46 miles) – will give you the best chance to meet Malay people, who live largely in the rural *kampungs* and fishing villages. The island is a blend of hilly rainforest and occasional plantations of rubber, oil palms, pepper, nutmeg, cloves and other spices. An island can be toured in a day, although overnight accommodation away from the beach resorts and George Town is limited.

About 15km (9½ miles) northwest of George Town are the resorts of **Batu Ferringhi** (Foreigner's Rock), with sandy beaches and rows of luxury resorts offering waterskiing, sailing, windsurfing, horse riding and other sports. There are also small hotels for travellers on a budget. The beaches may disappoint those who have travelled elsewhere in Malaysia.

Seaside fun at Batu Ferringhi

On a journey around the island, potential locations for stopovers are **Sungei Pinang** and **Pantai Aceh**, small Chinese villages reached by turning west off the main road. For fishing and snorkelling, stop at Teluk Bahang and hire a boat out to **Muka Head** on the island's northwest tip.

Alternatively, you could trek through the **Penang National Park**. The forest reserve covers some 20 sq km (8 sq miles) of the island's northwest corner. With only camping available as accommodation and vehicles denied access, the reward comes in possible sightings of wildlife like wild pigs, leopard-cats, slow loris, flying lemurs, leaf monkeys, macaques and black squirrels. The landscape is dotted with granite outcrops.

Near Teluk Bahang's town centre are the **Tropical Spice Garden** and **Penang Cultural Centre**; the latter features art and crafts and music and dance, as well as traditional architecture from elsewhere in Malaysia. At the southern end

A Malay *kampung* house made of wood, with a zinc roof

of Teluk Bahang village is the **Penang Butterfly Farm**, which has hundreds of different specimens fluttering around a netted enclosure of landscaped gardens.

A **tropical fruit farm**, just 8km (5 miles) from Teluk Bahang, has cultivated 140 types of exotic fruit trees on its 10 hectares (25 acres) since opening in 1992. Bird-watchers usually gather around **Genting**, about 3km (2 miles) from Balik Pulau, one of the world's largest nesting grounds for bee-eaters of all varieties – blue tailed, blue-throated, chestnut-headed and others flock here in their hundreds.

Snakes and smoke

Although the snakes in the Temple of the Azure Cloud are venomous, they are supposedly doped into a harmless state by the incense smoke. A few are said to have had their fangs pulled, and the monks will be happy to drape them around the shoulders of a camera-ready tourist.

As the road turns north again past the airport at Bayan Lepas, watch out for signs to the **Snake Temple**, more correctly known as the Temple of the Azure Cloud. Fifteen kilometres (9 miles) south from George Town, it was built in 1850 as a dedication to a Chinese monk, Chor Soo Kong, who gained fame through his ability to heal. After the temple was invaded by Wagler's vipers, it was decided they were incarnations of the monk and accorded sacred status.

North to Langkawi

Part of an archipelago of some 99 islands, the delightful resort island of Langkawi lies just south of the sea border to Thailand and, with its numerous hotels and resorts, is increasingly seen as Malaysia's premier island destination. For those travelling by road (rather than flying from KL), ferries leave from Kuala Perlis and Kuala Kedah. There are daily ferries from Penang and several per day to Satun in Southern Thailand. There are also flights to Langkawi from Singapore.

The Rice Bowl States

From Butterworth, the road stretching north into **Kedah State** heads into the rice bowl of Malaysia. Seas of green rice plants spread out on either side of the highway as it passes by the **Lembah Bujang** (Bujang Valley).

In the valley is an archaeological site that possibly dates back to a 5th-century Hindu kingdom called Langkasuka. The Indian traders may have used the city as an entrepôt with China. Buddhist temples have also been uncovered in the area.

Archaeologists are still uncovering remains on the southern slopes of **Gunung Jerai** (Kedah Peak). At 1,200m (3,936ft), this is the highest peak in Kedah. The Sungei Teroi Forest Recreation Park is to be found halfway up the mountain.

Via the towns of Sungai Petani and Bedong, a left turn takes you to **Merbok** to visit the **Candi Bukit Batu Pahat** (Temple of Chiselled Stone Hill). This is one of the 10th-century temples now reconstructed in the Lembah Bujang and possibly built by representatives of the South Indian Pallava dynasty before the 7th century BC. More artefacts, ceramics, *lingams* (phallic symbols), stone caskets, and gold and silver Shiva symbols are on show at Merbok's **Archaeological Museum**.

Beyond Gunung Jerai lie rice fields fed by the Muda River, which extend up to Perlis in the north and along the coastline from Penang to Langkawi. The Kedah State capital, **Alor Star**, is the last stop before the Thai border, and its history is a sad catalogue of invasion and subjugation, mostly by the Siamese (Thais). In the city centre is the traditional *padang* (square), dominated by the Crown of Kedah monument. The **Masjid Zahir**, built in 1912, stands on the square's western side. Opposite is the octagonal **Balai Nobat**, a tower where the royal instruments – drums, flutes and gongs – are stored. The **State Museum**, about 15 minutes by car just north of the city, was built in 1736, and is worth a visit for its collection of *Bunga Mas* and *Bunga*

Perak (flowers made of real gold and silver), sent to the ancient court of Siam as tribute.

The nearby port of **Kuala Kedah** is a departure point for ferries to Langkawi; you can see the remains of an 18th-century fort and sample some of Malaysia's best seafood.

Malaysia's smallest state, **Perlis**, also marks a change of scenery, from the flat rice lands to solitary limestone outcrops, many containing subterranean caves. The main towns are **Arau**, the royal town, and **Padang Besar**, where the Malaysian and Thai railways meet. From **Kuala Perlis**, south of the state capital, **Kangar**, it is a one-hour ferry journey to Langkawi and there are regular departures during the day.

Pulau Langkawi

The Langkawi archipelago, a cluster of 99 islands, some of which disappear under the high tide, has been a focal point

Datai Bay on the coast of Langkawi

Langkawi fisherfolk

in Malaysia's tourism promotion. Tourism in the area is centred on **Pulau Langkawi** and its array of some 20 international holiday resorts and hotels. For ferry travellers, **Kuah** is your arrival point, while those coming by air will land at the international airport, 18km (11 miles) northwest of the town. Kuah has some good Chinese, Thai, Indian and Malay restaurants and shops selling a range of goods at duty-free prices. Kuah's town square is dominated by a sculpture of a giant eagle (*langkawi* means red eagle in Malay). Next to the square is a theme park with 20 hectares (50 acres) of landscaped gardens.

It is possible to explore Langkawi's 80km (50 miles) of roads by hiring four-wheel-drive and standard cars, but many find bicycles and motorcycles a better alternative to reach parts of the island. The best beaches are Pantai Cenang, Pantai Tengah, Burau Bay and Datai Bay.

Most resort accommodation is located around Pantai Cenang on the island's southwestern tip, within easy reach of the international airport. These resorts include **Pelangi Beach Resort**, **Casa del Mar**, **Bon Ton** and the **Frangipani**. Other top resorts include the **Westin**, **Datai**, **Andaman**, **Four Seasons** and **Tanjung Rhu**. There are plenty of budget beach chalets located at Pantai Cenang and Pantai Tengah.

Underwater World at Pantai Cenang is reputed to be the largest aquarium in Southeast Asia, with over 5,000 marine and freshwater species. **Tasik Dayang Bunting** (Lake of the

Pregnant Maiden), the largest freshwater lake in the Langkawi islands is associated with the fable of a Kedah princess who drank the lake's water and became pregnant.

On the northern cape of Pulau Langkawi is **Tanjung Rhu**. From here a boat journey is the only way to reach the **Gua Cerita** (Cave of Legends) and the mangrove forests which are popular with ecotourists.

Other beaches to visit include **Pantai Kok**, **Pantai Tengah**, **Datai** and **Burau Bay**. Historical romantics may be interested to know that the islands were a favoured hideaway for the many pirates who preyed on ships in the Strait of Malacca.

Adventurous beach-goers might be interested in a **forest trek** across the middle of the island. Guided tours can be arranged for the hilly **Gunung Raya** and **Machincang Forest Reserves**, where a wide array of wildlife and birdlife can be seen. Riding the cable car to Mount Machincang provides views of Thailand. The mountain and other parts of the island form a Unesco geopark that protects the rocks, plants and animals.

Some 45 minutes south of Kuah by boat is **Pulau Singa Besar**, its 640 hectares (1,581 acres) of protected land a pleasant place to see native birds, animals and plants.

Other sites include a **Craft Cultural Complex** on the northern coast of Langkawi near Teluk Yu; and, near the airport, the **Atma Alam Batik Art Village**, a centre showcasing batik artists at work.

Langkawi legend

The absence of a detailed, legitimate history of Langkawi Island has led some to cultivate its mythology. One fable surrounds the death of Mahsuri. Her tomb, 12km (7 miles) west of Kuah, set amid a picturesque garden, pays tribute to a woman wrongly executed for adultery more than 200 years ago. As legend has it, she bled white blood, a testament to her innocence, and in her dying words cursed the island for seven generations.

THE EAST COAST AND JOHOR

Malaysia's less-visited east coast offers visitors a slower pace, set against the beauty of the region's beaches and the richness of its forests. The region covers four states – **Kelantan**, **Terengganu**, **Pahang** and **Johor** – with most road traffic plying the coastal road between Kota Bharu, close to the Thai border, and Johor Bahru, just a causeway's distance from Singapore. Historically resistant to many of the major changes in the rest of Malaysia, the region has been able to maintain its authentic Malay culture and Islamic traditions.

> ### Kampung crafts
>
> Traditional handicrafts, including the making of spinning tops, kites, silverware, baskets and batik, are still practised in many of the rural *kampung* in Kelantan and Terengganu.

The east coast's beaches are less developed and offer opportunities for snorkelling and diving. Wildlife enthusiasts can enter the forests for jungle trekking and adventure travel. The region also offers the chance to see leatherback turtles coming to lay their eggs at Cherating and Ma'Daerah near Kuantan; and to view the artisans at Kuala Terengganu, whose boat-building skills are legendary.

Economic growth and prosperity – through the discovery of oil offshore from Terengganu – has led to more resorts opening, offering a wider range of accommodation at competitive rates.

Kelantan

White sandy beaches stretch north from the state capital, Kota Bharu, to the Thai border. Buddhist temples close to the capital hark back to the time when Kelantan was under the influence of Siamese kings. The British colonial influence here, which came into being in a 1909 agreement with Siam, only lasted three decades before their defeat by the Japanese in World War II. Kelantan's isolation, as well as its embrace of Islam in the 17th century, kept British colonialism and economic change at bay during the 19th century and enabled this cradle of Malay culture to remain intact.

Here you will see soaring decorative kites as well as the *wayang kulit* (shadow puppet shows), dating back to when Kelantan was influenced by the kingdom of Funan in Indochina some 2,000 years ago.

Known as the 'Land of Lightning' – due to the heavy storms during the wet season of November to February – Kelantan's gateway is Kota Bharu, just 40 minutes by air from Kuala Lumpur and only 30km (19 miles) from the Thai border. To the south, where towns dot the main highway, are points of access to the many beaches and fishing villages, which are at the heart of the region's economy and culture.

Boat-building is among the traditional crafts practised in Kelantan

Kota Bharu

Set upon the banks of the Kelantan River, Kota Bahru's key attractions are close to the **Pasar Besar** (Central Market) on Jalan Doktor. Here rows of food and farm produce resemble works of art, with vegetables, fruit and meat on the ground level and kitchenware, baskets and other goods on the floors above.

The **Buluh Kubu Bazaar** is good for bargain-hunters seeking T-shirts or silverware. Silversmiths are also found on **Jalan Sultanah Zainab**, while batik and other cottage-industry goods are found over the Jalan Wakat Mek Zainab bridge. The **night market**, near Pasar Besar, provides worthwhile evening entertainment and gives visitors a chance to savour Kelantanese food.

At sundown, riverside restaurants also come to life near to **Padang Merdeka** (Independence Square), now an open

Fresh produce in Kota Bharu's Central Market

park area for recreation but once the town's fresh produce market. Merdeka Square was the site where the body of slain Malay warrior Tok Janggut (Father Long Beard), who led a rebellion against the British in the early years of the century, was exhibited in 1915. The Declaration of Independence was read here on 31 August 1957.

Batik-making involves colourful and intricate design

Across the square is the **War Museum**, housed in the building used by the Japanese Army as their headquarters during World War II. Next door is the **Muzium Islam** (Islamic Museum), and the ornate **Masjid Negeri** (State Mosque) beyond.

The **Istana Jahar** (Royal Customs Museum) was built in 1887, with additions by Sultan Muhamad IV in the early years of the 20th century. The **Istana Balai Besar** (Palace with the Large Audience Hall) was built in 1840 under Sultan Muhamad II and is now only opened on ceremonial occasions (for invited guests).

On the other side of town, along Jalan Hospital, near the Tourist Information Centre, is the **Kelantan State Museum**, displaying rural Malay artwork and earthenware pots. The best view of living Malaysian culture is to be seen at the **Gelanggang Seni** (Culture Centre) on Jalan Mahmood opposite the Perdana Hotel, with performances that include *wayang kulit*, *main gasing* (top spinning) and *silat* (self defence), except on Fridays and during Ramadan.

Around Kota Bharu

Within just a few kilometres of Kota Bharu, visitors can find master silversmiths and expert batik-makers, but the maze of country lanes around the town could make it difficult to find the *kampung* communities where the artisans still use their traditional skills. A guide can be recommended by the Tourist Information Centre.

Kelantan's silversmiths use two techniques, the 'filigree' and '*repoussé*', and items range from the purely ornamental to the functional. Silver-craft factories can be visited at **Kampung Sireh**, along Jalan Sultanah Zainab, **Kampung Marak** and **Kampung Badang**, as well as on the road to Pantai Cahaya Bulan (PCB). Also on the way to PCB, visitors can see the skill and beauty of *kain songket*, richly woven materials of gold and silver thread, at **Kampung Penambang**. Songket was the product of the region's early trade with

Preparing to fly a colourful kite or *wau*

China (silk) and India (gold and silver thread). Batik-makers are found throughout the state, but there are bigger factories to be found at **Kampung Puteh**, **Kubur Kuda** and **Kampung Badang** near the city.

Kite-makers also practise their age-old skills throughout the region, and while tradition would have the art passed from father to son, many fear the younger generation now lacks the patience to carry out the skilled handiwork required.

One of the oldest mosques in Malaysia is found at **Nilam Puri**. It was dismantled and taken from a site closer to the river at Kampung Laut in 1968, after repeated flooding. The mosque was built entirely without the use of nails. It is now a centre for religious studies and only open to Muslims.

Kelantan's ancient links with Thailand are evident in the number of **Thai Buddhist Temples** you will see half-hidden among the groves of palm and laurel, rising above the rice paddies. North of the estuary of the Kelantan River near **Tumpat** (12km/7 miles from town) is one of the most important of these temples, **Wat Phothivihan**, which is noted for its 40m (130ft) reclining Buddha. At **Kampung Perasit**, south of Kota Bharu, is **Wat Putharamaram**.

A significant landmark of World War II can be visited at **Sabak Beach**, 13km (8 miles) northwest of Kota Bharu, near the mouth of the Kelantan River. Here is the site of the first Japanese assault in the Pacific War, just over an hour before Pearl Harbor was bombed *(see page 24)*. Jutting out of the sandy beach in the pleasant shade of palm and casuarina trees stands a crumbling bunker that the Indian artillery defended to the last soldier.

The Beaches

Kelantan's white sandy beaches are easily reached from Kota Bharu and provide plenty of opportunities for a pleasant swim. Most popular is **Pantai Cahaya Bulan**, or Moonlight Beach. It was previously known as Pantai Cinta Berahi, the Beach of Passionate Love, a somewhat incongruous name in this strict Muslim region where *khalwat,* or close proximity between sexes, is prohibited. It is 10km (6 miles) north of the town, one reason why it is so popular during weekends and holidays.

Pantai Seri Tujuh (Beach of the Seven Lagoons), about 7km (4 miles) from Kota Bharu, is the venue for the International Kite Festival and lies on the border with Thailand.

To the south, **Pantai Irama** (Melody Beach) is some 25km (16 miles) from Kota Bharu; it is one of the most beautiful along the entire coast. On the journey to Terengganu is **Pantai Bisikan Bayu** (Beach of the Whispering Breeze, also known as Pantai Dalam Rhu). Stop off at the fishing village of **Semerak**, 19km (12 miles) from Pasir Puteh, where you can buy excellent seafood for a barbecue on the beach.

Terengganu

A coast of sandy beaches along the 225km (140 miles) of landfall facing the South China Sea, not to mention several offshore islands and hinterland forests near Tasik (Lake) Kenyir, give Terengganu its appeal. The wealth from offshore oil discoveries in recent years has buoyed the state, something you'll see reflected in the skyline and busy traffic of the capital, Kuala Terengganu. So far the economic gains have failed to detract from the town's relaxed charm. The main options for travelling to Terengganu are direct flights from KL or interstate buses to Kuala Terengganu, which is generally the starting point for a trip to the island resorts or to Tasik Kenyir.

The Islands

The islands off Terengganu's north coast are accessible from both Kuala Terengganu or by way of the fishing village of **Kuala Besut**, 45km (28 miles) south of Kota Bharu, which is the departure point to Pulau Perhentian's islands. Before leaving Kuala Besut, you could visit **Bukit Keluang**, just on the coast, for watersports and some easily accessible caves.

The islands of **Pulau Perhentian Kecil** and **Pulau Perhentian Besar** are reached after a 21km (13-mile) journey which takes up to two hours. The islands' main appeal is that they are lush and tropical, with clear blue waters and coral reefs protected as part of Malaysia's marine park network. On both islands, accommodation ranges from good resorts to chalets.

South from Pulau Perhentian Besar lies **Pulau Redang**, some 50km (31 miles) off the coast. Its nine islands make up

Lake Kenyir, Terengganu

the largest of Terengganu's archipelagoes. It is also developing quickly and is strongly promoted by travel agents in Kuala Terengganu, but there is still the promise of clear waters for scuba diving. The journey to the islands takes two hours from the village of **Merang** (not to be confused with the town of **Marang** further south). There are also resorts on **Pulau Lang Tengah**, just west of the Redang Islands. Boats take 45 minutes to reach the island from Merang.

Kuala Terengganu

The lively state capital of **Kuala Terengganu**, bordered by the Terengganu River and the South China Sea, is the largest town in the state and has progressed from a sleepy fishing village to a bustling, colourful centre. Aside from the beautiful **Masjid Tengku Tengah Zaharah**, 4½km (3 miles) out of town, most sites of interest are along the town's waterfront. The mosque, built on an estuary of the Ibai River, gives the illusion that it is floating on water.

Sunset at Kuala Terengganu

Back in town, a waterfront stroll leads through **Chinatown** on Jalan Bandar. The old terraced buildings on both sides of the road create an attractive sense of timelessness even as the betting shops do a lively afternoon trade. Jalan Bandar leads you to the **Pasar Besar Kedai Payang** (Central Market), a multi-level complex attached to a car park, with a fruit, vegetable and fish market on the ground floor and local textiles and handicrafts above.

A short river cruise from the jetty, **Pulau Duyung Besar** is a little island of boat-builders, whose reputations extend far beyond Malaysia. Late in the year, the Monsoon Cup sailing race is staged off the island in the blustery monsoon breezes.

Several other attractions are located outside the town. Opposite Pulau Sekati, 5km (3 miles) from town – but also accessible from the river – is the **Terengganu State Museum**, in a traditionally styled complex of four blocks housing 10 galleries at Bukit Losong. The largest state museum in Malaysia, its galleries are dedicated to maritime exhibits, traditional architecture, Islamic arts, textiles, crafts, and royal regalia. For local silk weaving, try the **Sutera Semai Centre** at Chendering, 6km (3 miles) from Kuala Terengganu, where visitors can see different stages of silk-making and batik-painting. Also on offer is *songket*, woven with silver and gold threads, and brassware.

Around Kuala Terengganu

Fifty-five kilometres (34 miles) inland from Kuala Terengganu is the largest constructed lake in Southeast Asia, **Tasik Kenyir**, which was created by flooding the valley to construct the country's largest hydroelectric dam, completed in 1985. For anglers looking for freshwater fish, the waters of Tasik Kenyir, covering an area of 37,000 hectares (91,400 acres) and 340 islands, are the place to go. There is also an adventurous trail to **Taman Negara**. Besides fishing, jet skiing, windsurfing, canoeing and jungle trekking are all available.

There are also several waterfalls, rapids and cascades within the lake region, including the **Sekayu Waterfalls**, just 56km (35 miles) west of Kuala Terengganu. After trekking through the rainforest, you can enjoy a swim in one of the many natural pools created among the rocks by the cascading river.

Marang is a fishing village 15km (9 miles) south of Kuala Terengganu. Here, and across the long wooden bridge at **Patah Malam**, you may see fishermen mending their nets in the shade of coconut palms. Marang provides access to the island of **Pulau Kapas** which, though less than 2km (1 mile) in length, is considered one of the finest islands on the east coast. There are several resorts and chalet accommodation on the island.

Ma'Daerah Turtle Sanctuary Centre

Turtle watching at Rantau Abang was once the cornerstone of tourism in Terengganu. The Turtle and Marine Ecosystem Centre here released around half a million hatchlings between

Save the Turtles

In the years before ecological awareness, many onlookers treated the turtles' rendezvous as a popular spectacle. Crowds gathered in festive mood to build campfires on the beach, dance to loud music, take pictures by blinding flashlight of the turtles' night-time egg laying, even ride the backs of the leatherback turtles and poke open their heavy-lidded eyes. This irresponsibility almost put a stop to the natural phenomenon. The annual number of leatherbacks visiting Rantau Abang declined from about 2,000 in the 1950s to barely a few hundred by the end of the 1980s. At this point, the Malaysian Fisheries Department stepped in. Authorities have banned the use of flash photography or flashlights, and visitors must stay 5m (15ft) from the turtles. Despite this, in 2007 just one leatherback laid its eggs at Rantau Abang. The situation at Ma'Daerah (see above) is far more encouraging.

1975 and 2005. However, while all four turtle species found in the state are protected, in 2007 just one leatherback turtle landed and laid eggs in a beachside nest at Rantau Abang.

The dramatic decline in nesting turtles over the past decade has inevitably led to a drop in tourists visiting Rantau Abang, but there was renewed hope with the establishment in 1999 of the **Ma'Daerah Turtle Sanctuary Centre**, 10km north of Kemaman. Malaysia's World Wide Fund for Nature (WWF) was instrumental in seeking support from the government and the State

Measuring a visiting leatherback

Fisheries Department, as well as from industry and the local community to establish a nature education centre to generate awareness about the plight of turtles, and in particular that of the endangered leatherback turtle.

The centre provides hatchery facilities on the beach at Ma'-Daerah, runs children's environmental camps, produces information booklets, organises beach clean-ups and holds talks with local fishing villagers to eliminate illegal fishing gear that can kill turtles.

Tanjung Jara and Points South

The highway south from Rantau Abang, heading towards Kuantan, the state capital of Pahang, passes through **Tanjung**

Jara. Here, the award-winning accommodation of the Tanjung Jara Resort contrasts with the industrialisation from the region's offshore oil and gas exploration. Further south is **Kuala Dungun**, which is predominantly Chinese in character and offers excellent cuisine. From here you can hire a boat to the island of **Pulau Tenggol**, 30km (18 miles) offshore, where you can go swimming and snorkelling among the angelfish. The centre of Terengganu's petroleum industry is **Kerteh**, with its refineries and gasworks. But there are some picturesque beaches at the mouth of the Kerteh River nonetheless.

A peaceful vista at the beach resort of Cherating

Pahang

The largest state in the peninsula has the longest river, the 475km (296-mile) long Pahang. Although its most famous sights lie to the west in the Genting and Cameron Highlands, Pahang has beach resorts including the renowned Pulau Tioman (Tioman Island) in the far south (though access by sea is from Mersing in Johor). Endau-Rompin National Park, straddling the border with Johor state, complements the better known Taman Negara in the far north, which has road access through the state capital Kuantan. Tasik Chini is a scenic lake, but has limited tourism facilities.

The Coast

Just 47km (30 miles) from Kuantan is the beach resort area of **Cherating**, where Club Méditerranée set up its first resort in Asia. But Club Med is not alone along the beachfront. Other resorts in close proximity to the state's capital are located at **Balok Beach**. The Hyatt Resort Kuantan has joined other resorts at the **Teluk Chempedak Beach**, only 5km (3 miles) out of the bustling city. The beautiful **Pelindung Beach** is just a short trek through the Teluk Chempedak Forest Reserve. From May to September, green turtles and the occasional leatherback turtle may be seen under moonlit skies when they lay their eggs on the beach. At the **Beserah Beach**, also close to Kuantan, local fishermen still employ buffalo to pull the carts carrying their catch to the market. A batik factory and several cottage handicraft workshops here may disappoint more sophisticated souvenir-hunters. You will find a pleasant beach nearby at **Batu Hitam**.

Kuantan

Kuantan township offers a wide range of hotels, a lively shopping and market quarter, and a quiet ambience next to the river where good food stalls are found. Built on the fortunes from tin mining, the capital is now a commercial centre for Pahang's oil, palm and other industries, and a key link in the east coast petroleum and gas pipelines.

There are no international hotels in the city but MS Garden International and Swiss Garden both have good standards. On the same street, Jalan Masjid, is the cultural centre (**Infokraf**), and just opposite is an open sports field. The area around Jalan A. Aziz and Jalan Besar has many shops, warehouses and the occasional money-lender. The local village of **Selamat** is known for its fine *kain songket* silk brocade.

Pekan

The sleepy old royal capital of Pahang, 45km (28 miles) south of Kuantan, is home to the sultan's palace, **Istana Abu Bakar**, set upstream on the Pahang River among immaculate polo fields. Gilded and sapphire-blue domes grace two marble mosques and the **Sultan's Mausoleum**. Nearby, the Victorian **State Museum** displays glories of the old sultanate and treasures from a Chinese junk salvaged from the South China Sea. The town also has a silk-weaving centre at **Kampung Pulau Keladi**, 5km (3 miles) from Pekan.

The home of the Sultan of Pekan

Tasik Chini

Comprising a dozen beautiful lakes surrounded by forested hills, **Tasik Chini** is situated south of the Pahang River, 100km (60 miles) west of Kuantan. From August to September, much of the surface is covered by white lotus blossoms. The lakes are said to be the home of giant snakes, dragons and other mythical monsters, one of which, according to local myth, swam to the South China Sea and became Tioman Island. Archaeological explorations suggest there are ruins of a Khmer settlement beneath the surface. Outside the lotus-flowering season, the lakes are still a delight to visit, with good fishing for *toman*. Members of the Jakun tribe dwell on the lake's shore. It may be possible to visit **Kampung Gumum**, one of their hamlets.

Tioman Island

The combination of first-rate resort facilities and magnificent natural beauty makes **Tioman Island** one of the finest in Asia. Preserved from logging, most of the rainforest has remained. A hilly ridge runs down the middle of the island at an altitude of 500m (1,640ft), rising at the southern end to two granite peaks – the Donkey's Ears. The taller of these, Mount Kajang, is 1,038m (3,405ft) high.

You can reach Tioman by flying from Kuala Lumpur (Subang Jaya Airport) or by boat from the fishing village of Mersing. It takes two hours to reach Tioman by express boat.

On the island's west coast, choose between the **Berjaya Tioman Golf and Spa Resort** and the modest but comfortable guest-houses, chalets and simpler cabins on **Salang Beach** further north. Facilities around the main island port of **Tekek** include restaurants, diving shops and a golf course. For an exclusive experience, Japa Mala is a private beachside retreat.

Most trips around the island are by boat, and the fishermen charge a reasonable fee. From Tekek, make the **forest trek** over the hill to the east coast. Take a dip at the hilltop waterfall, then make your way down to the beach at **Juara**, a village serving excellent seafood. Have another swim in the sea, and if you do not feel like trekking back, return to Tekek by boat.

Birdwatchers may see pied imperial pigeons, bulbuls, frigate birds, sunbirds and flower-peckers. Characteristically for island forests, there are no large mammals. There have been some recent reptile discoveries.

Johor

Proximity to Singapore has buoyed the economy of Johor, the peninsula's southernmost state, and that of its capital, Johor Bahru. Easy access from Singapore to east-coast resorts like Desaru and Sebana Cove in the southeast and the islands offshore from Mersing has also increased development of these destinations. Johor's links to Singapore have renewed its position as a guardian of Malay culture since it first provided a refuge in the 16th century for the banished royal court of Melaka. Johor offers many opportunities for tourism, from shopping to motor racing, horse riding to water sports, and adventure travel in the Endau-Rompin National Park. These relatively untouched forests at the border with Pahang delight ecotourists.

The Endau-Rompin National Park

Straddling the Johor and Pahang border, **Endau-Rompin National Park**'s 870 sq km (336 sq miles) of forest and rivers is fast gaining a reputation among travellers as an alternative to the more established Taman Negara. The park is home to the Malayan tiger, Asian elephant, wild boar and the largest surviving population of Sumatran rhinoceros in Peninsular Malaysia. Other species to be found here include the *binturong* (bear cat) and the white-handed gibbon, the only ape species in the region. Among the birdlife are drongos, many species of hornbill and great argus pheasants. Endau-Rompin is also home to the Orang Asli of the Jakun tribe.

Much less developed than the parks of Sarawak and Sabah – and so far more pristine – Endau-Rompin offers a rare challenge to adventurous travellers. Facilities for accommodation are limited to chalets, dormitories and three campsites in the park, located at **Batu Hampar**, **Upeh Guling** and **Buaya Sangkut**. You must employ a guide or go on a group tour.

From Johor Bahru, travel by the North–South Expressway to Keluang, and take a detour to Kahang town. From there, only a four-wheel-drive vehicle will take you along the 56km (35-mile) jungle track to Kampung Peta, where there is a visitor centre and point of entry to the national park. Otherwise, you can get there via a three-hour boat journey from Felda Nitar II. There is controlled entry and quite strident regulations governing park usage and duration periods.

Desaru and the Islands North

The southeast corner of the peninsula was originally used for oil-palm plantations. Today, tourism helps the economy, and its high-class hotels share 25km (15 miles) of golden sands. **Desaru** is accessible by road via **Kota Tinggi**, or by following the coast road from Johor Bahru. If travelling through Kota Tinggi, it might be worthwhile making a stopover to see the **waterfall** at **Lombong**, 15km (9½ miles) north of the town centre. Desaru is 52km (32 miles) further east and is the first major beach resort for Singaporeans. There are several premier resorts and golf courses here, including Sebana Cove, Desaru Golden Beach Hotel and the Desaru View Golf and Country Club, but budget travellers will also find reasonable value chalet accommodation available.

Off the coast from the resorts of **Mersing**, there are several islands – **Pulau Rawa**, **Pulau Tengah**, **Pulau Besar**,

Following a river trail in the Endau-Rompin National Park

Pulau Tinggi and **Pulau Sibu** – offering white sandy beaches, coral reefs and budget accommodation. Boats can be hired from Mersing to take you out to one of the more secluded islands.

Johor Bahru

Citizens of Singapore cross the causeway to Johor's state capital to escape for the weekend and sample its lively nightlife, to shop, or to head further north. Outside the restaurants and malls, travellers can visit the sprawling **market**, and nearby along the **Lido Waterfront** take a look at the gleaming white marble of the **Sultan Abu Bakar Mosque**, the **Royal Museum** and the **Istana Gardens** of the old palace, with its Japanese tea house and the sultan's private zoo, which is now open to the public.

The neoclassical **Istana Besar Palace** is now used for state ceremonies, the present-day sultans having moved further north to the modern **Istana Bukit Serene**, with a 32m (104ft) high tower. Other sights include the colonial-style clock tower overlooking the **Dataran Bandaraya** (City Square). The Johor Art Gallery, built in 1910 in a similar period style, exhibits clothing, weapons, currency and manuscripts, as well as examples of calligraphy and ceramic items, along with artworks.

North Towards Melaka

Two roads – Jalan Tun Dr Ismail and Jalan Tun Abdul Razak – lead northwards out of Johor Bahru to the west coast. The Second Crossing is a new bridge from the western side of Singapore into Johor. Not far from Taman Tasik they merge into one in the direction of Ayer Hitam. Before heading towards Melaka, turn west at Skudai to the coast road and back south to **Kukup**, a fishing village 40km (25 miles) southwest of Johor Bahru.

At **Ayer Hitam**, a wide range of Chinese-style pottery is on display beside the fruit market. The market town of **Batu Pahat** also offers respectable Chinese restaurants. The town witnessed a historic Melaka naval victory over the Siamese fleet in 1456. The fishing port of **Muar** was of trading importance to the British in the 19th century, as can be seen in the graceful old neoclassical government offices. It was here that Australian troops made an heroic last stand against the Japanese advance on Singapore in January 1942.

A diver's paradise

SARAWAK AND SABAH

From rainforests to mountains, the states of Sarawak and Sabah offer enough adventure and natural beauty to make the journey across the South China Sea worthwhile. Images of cloud-engulfed mountain-tops, a tattooed and decorated member of the Iban tribe at a riverside longhouse, a bustling produce market, a beachside retreat bordering on turquoise waters, or an orang-utan sitting in a lazy pose all mark sides of the genuine adventure which awaits travellers to East Malaysia. From shopping for exotic souvenirs and craftwork to dining in seaside restaurants to the thrill of riding in a longboat along river 'highways' deep in the forests, it is all there for the choosing.

A Dayak woman

Music festivals in Sarawak such as Rainforest World Music and Miri Jazz add a cultural dimension.

Historic evidence of the 'White Rajah' – the lineage that commenced with adventurer James Brooke in the 1830s and lasted until the start of World War II – can still be seen in Kuching, Sarawak's capital.

Away from the cities lie some natural treasures: Borneo's highest mountain (Mount Kinabalu in Sabah), its longest river (the Rejang in Sarawak), its many caves (including the Niah and Mulu Caves in Sarawak), and natural parks with wonderful wildlife and flora. For a change of pace, there are plenty of beaches along the southern and eastern coasts and lots of islands for snorkelling or turtle-watching.

Getting around can be a challenge. The rivers, more numerous and much longer than on the peninsula, still provide the principal way into the interior, supplemented by smaller aircraft operated by Malaysia Airlines (MASwings).

Sarawak

It is just 90 minutes by air from Kuala Lumpur to Kuching, the historic capital of Malaysia's largest state – covering 124,967 sq km (48,250 sq miles). From the air you'll be able to see that Sarawak has the country's longest river, the

Rejang, flowing 563km (350 miles) from the mountains on the Indonesian border to the South China Sea. The wealth of river systems among the forest terrain provides a vital link that will transport you to the tribes of the rainforest. Between taking river cruises or treks through the rainforest of Bako National Park, you can relax at the beachside of Santubong and Damai, just 40 minutes from Kuching. In eastern Sarawak, you can pursue more strenuous but exhilarating adventures in the Niah or Mulu cave systems.

Sarawak and Sabah operate their own immigration and visitors from the mainland are required to produce their passports.

Aborigines of Northern Borneo

These many tribes were once collectively known as Land or Sea Dayaks.

Iban, the largest indigenous group in Sarawak, dwell in longhouses along lowland river banks. They farm rice, rubber and pepper.

Melanau inhabit the coastal plain east of Kuching, where they fish and grow cassava.

Bidayuh, the original Land Dayaks who allied with the White Rajahs of the 19th century, are longhouse dwellers of western Sarawak.

Kenyah and Kayan are two distinct tribes but often live side by side along the upper reaches of Sarawak's Baram and Rejang rivers. They farm hill rice and rubber, and rear pigs and poultry.

Penan, the last of East Malaysia's nomads, stay upriver well clear of civilisation. The men make superb weapons – machetes and blowpipes – and the women are renowned as basket-weavers.

Kadazan/Dusun, Sabah's biggest tribe, have adapted smoothly to urban life – and Christianity – in Kota Kinabalu. Others live on terraced hills around Mount Kinabulu.

Bajau are Muslim seafarers affectionately known as 'Sea Gypsies'. Their land-lubber cousins are admired as daring cowboy cattle-breeders.

Murut are hunters in the hill country along the Sabah–Sarawak border.

Kuching

Unlike the other major towns of East Malaysia – Miri, Kota Kinabalu and Sandakan – Sarawak's state capital has preserved its colonial charm, having been spared from the bombs of World War II. **Kuching** is built on a bend of the Sarawak River, 32km (20 miles) from the sea. The residence and fort built by the White Rajahs *(see page 22)* lie on the north bank, while on the southern bank is the greater part of the town, including Chinese and Indian merchants, major hotels and several colonial buildings, permanent vestiges of the past.

The colonial buildings include the **General Post Office**, noteworthy for its 1930s neoclassical design and pillars, and the **Courthouse**. The courthouse site was originally a German Lutheran mission before James Brooke, the first of the White Rajahs, turned it into a judicial administration office. In 1858 that building was demolished, making way for a second and later a third structure (the one that still stands), which was completed in 1874. State Council meetings continued to be held there until 1973. Today it houses the **Sarawak Tourism Complex**. The clock tower, whose bells still chime on the hour, was added in 1883. In front of the courthouse is the **Charles Brooke Memorial**, 6m (20ft) in height, which was built in 1924 in remembrance of the second White Rajah.

Along the **Waterfront**, north of the courthouse, is the **Square Tower**, with an information centre and multimedia theatre on its ground floor.

West of the Courthouse is **Jalan India**, a pedestrian mall marking the city's Muslim centre. Sarawak's oldest **Indian Mosque**, built in the 1850s, is here. Still further west, the **Kuching Mosque**, built in 1968 near the markets, is best seen from the other side of the river. A new mosque has also been built on the north side of the river.

The main **Central Market** is located on Jalan Gambier, near the Waterfront. Here fresh fish, poultry and vegetables are sold, as well as clothes, newspapers and DVDs. Nearby are the bus terminal and taxi stand.

Despite new high-rise constructions, the numerous traditional shophouses – both Chinese and Indian – ensure the city's heritage is still within reach. Chinese shophouses along **Jalan Padungan**, mostly built during the rubber boom of the 1920s and 1930s, offer a variety of restaurants, coffee houses and handicraft shops.

More colourful is the **Sunday Market** on Jalan Satok at Jalan Palm, which actually starts late on Saturday afternoon and extends through Sunday morning, offering a bewildering array of items; Dayaks come to sell fruit, vegetables and handicrafts and even more exotic items from the forest. Clothes and household goods appeal to the locals.

East of the Courthouse, the **Tua Pek Kong Temple** and the **Chinese History Museum** are near a group of five-star

The Kuching Waterfront

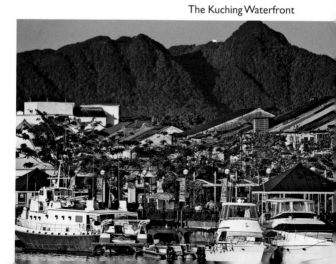

hotels that line the river. The temple, also known as the Siew San Teng Temple, was built in 1876 and is the oldest in Kuching; it remains an active place of worship. The nearby museum traces the long history of the Chinese in Sarawak, who lived there well before the arrival of James Brooke. Another temple is the **Kuek Seng Ong Temple**, on Lebuh Wayang, built in 1895. Finally, the **Lim Fah San Monastery Association** is located on Jalan Sampang Tua.

For a small fee, venture across the Sarawak River by *tambang* (ferry) to view the **Astana** (1870) and recently renovated **Fort Margherita** (1879). The Astana (which means palace in Malay), was originally the Brooke family's home. It comprises three bungalows under a single roof and is built off the ground, supported by brick pillars. The building has a library and a collection of artefacts associated with the Brooke family. The ground floor was the location for many garden parties hosted by the Rajahs; it was also used as an internment centre for Japanese prisoners of war in World War II. It is now the residence of the Governor of Kuching, the Yang Di-Pertua Negeri. Set among beautiful grounds, it is, unfortunately, not open to the public.

Up the hill to the right from the Astana, the road leads to Fort Margherita, which used to house the Muzium Polis. The white-turreted edifice was built by Sir Charles Brooke along the lines of an English medieval castle and named after his

Catcall

The town's name is said to have been given it by James Brooke, the first White Rajah, when a cat, *kuching* in Malay, ran across the room during a conference with local chiefs. The legend has been enough to justify a whole room being given over to cats at the Sarawak Museum, cat statues and a Cat Museum.

wife, Margaret. It was converted to a police museum in 1971, but this was closed in 2004. The views from here across the river to the city are most pleasant and the journey across the river on a small and colourful *tambang* has to be one of the last great river crossings in the whole of Southeast Asia. The boats depart from along the Waterfront.

On the south side of the river, another colonial building is the **Round Tower** on Jalan Tun Abang Haji Openg. It was originally designed as a dispensary when built in the 1880s.

Crossing the river by *tambang*

Also south of the river on Jalan Tun Haji Openg is the **Sarawak Museum**, which has one of the best collections of folk art and flora and fauna in Southeast Asia. The museum is divided between the old and new wings, connected by a footbridge across the road. The former was built in 1891 and styled along the lines of a Normandy townhouse; it is devoted to Sarawak's rich history and diverse cultures. Another wing, completed in 1983, has more galleries and archaeological exhibits, including a reconstruction of early human settlements at the Niah Caves. There is a book and souvenir shop.

Within the museum's grounds are the **Botanic Gardens** and the **Heroes Memorial**, the latter commemorating the dead from World War II, the Communist Emergency and the

Tribal art at Sarawak Museum

Confrontation with Indonesia. Adjacent to the new wing of the Sarawak Museum is the **Muzium Islam** (Islamic Museum) with its seven galleries.

Highlights of the old wing include a reconstructed **Iban Longhouse**, complete with totem-pole, hornbill-feather headdresses and skulls of head-hunting victims; the **Kenyah Tree of Life Mural**, repainted from one at a longhouse at Long Nawang; **Melanau dolls**, which serve as charms against disease and to lure animals to traps; and specimens of Alfred Russel Wallace's extensive collection of insects.

The new wing is home to galleries of **Hindu and Buddhist sculptures**; Chinese, Thai, Japanese and European **ceramics** and **brassware**; a model of the **Niah Caves** *(see page 113)*, with their birds, bats and other fauna, and Stone Age artefacts and funeral boats from the 8th century AD. A photographic history of Kuching is also interesting.

One gallery has become the world's first **Cat Museum**, in honour of the city's feline mascot *(see page 106)*.

Around Kuching

The fishing village and peninsula of **Santubong** is 40 minutes from Kuching. There you will find beach resorts and cultural sights, plus trails for forest trekking, bike riding and golf.

Mount Santubong (810m/2,655ft) peers down on **Damai**, where you will find beach-side resorts. Nearby is the **Sarawak Cultural Village**, 7 hectares (17 acres) of craft demonstrations and cultural performances. Described as a 'living museum', it provides an opportunity to learn about Sarawak's rich culture. In July each year the village comes alive with the Sarawak Rainforest World Music Festival, a celebration of music and friendship.

There are three beach resorts and a rainforest resort at Damai, each offering a range of water sports, jungle trekking trips and cultural activities. Two of the resorts, both located at **Teluk Penyu Beach**, are within easy reach of the Cultural Village. Outside the village, there is access to local longhouses as well as trips to the Bako National Park, local fishing villages and nearby islands and river cruises and dolphin-spotting expeditions around the Santubong Peninsula.

In Sarawak two major centres are involved with orangutan rehabilitation. **Semengoh Orang-Utan Sanctuary**, southwest of Kuching, rehabilitates orphaned babies and adults who have been kept as domestic pets. At **Matang Wildlife Centre**, northwest of Kuching. while the focus of their work is on the orang-utans, there are also enclosures for sambar deer, crocodiles, sun bears, civets and bear cats, as well as aviaries holding hornbills, sea eagles and other birdlife from Sarawak.

Bako National Park

Both **Bako National Park** and **Kubah National Park** are within easy reach of Kuching. Sarawak's oldest national park, Bako is also one of the smallest, covering just 27 sq km (10 sq miles), but it offers great opportunities to see a wide range of animal and plant life. Since the park is located just one hour (37km/23 miles) from Kuching, visitors have a choice between a day trip or an overnight stay;

Iban cultural dance

accommodation includes dormitories and chalets. You must first travel to Kampung Bako, where you can get a boat to transport you to the park headquarters at Telok Assam. The paunchy **proboscis monkey** with its long nose is the major attraction, but you can also see silver-leaf monkeys and long-tail macaques as well as mousedeer, monitor lizards and a variety of birdlife.

At Bako there are 16 well-marked, colour-coded jungle trails with bridges over the swamps to the best spots for viewing flora and wildlife. Twelve of the trails lead off from the right of the park's headquarters, just across from the arrival jetty. The **Jalan Tanjong Sapi**, a 30-minute steep climb up to the cliff-tops overlooking the bay that fronts the park headquarters, is recommended.

On the Jalan Lintang, a small observation hide at the **Lintang Salt Lick** offers the chance to see the animals at close quarters as they drink. Besides its good hilltop view over the forest, the **Bukit Tambi Trail** is home to several specimens of carnivorous plants: the bladderwort, pitcher plant and sundew (Venus flytrap).

Telok Delima and **Telok Paku trails** are the best paths for viewing the proboscis monkeys as they like to bed down in trees near the seashore. Very often, they will have been watching you long before you spot them, and if your presence upsets them, they will just honk and disappear. Along the seashore, keep a look out for hairy-nosed otters.

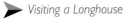

Visiting a Longhouse

The opportunity to see the tribes of Sarawak in their forest homes is a privilege not to be missed. However, tours to some longhouses have acquired the artificial character of a 'tribal theme park'. As tourism grows and the popularity of such expeditions increases, it is a trend difficult to escape, the only real alternative being to travel even further into the forests at added expense. But the adoption by some villagers of Western clothing or items like televisions and radios shouldn't put you off.

On offer for adventurous travellers is a choice between a day trip, an overnight stay at a guesthouse near a longhouse, or a stay in a longhouse itself. Tours from Kuching usually start very

Life in the Longhouse

A typical longhouse is a communal dwelling of perhaps 20 'apartments', attached one to the other and extended as each family adds a unit of parents with children. Erected close to the river, it is built of sturdy, axe-hewn timber, preferably Sarawak's coveted *belian* ironwood. The structure is raised above the ground on massive pillars – a technique evolved in the past to resist enemy attacks rather than mere river flooding.

A notched tree trunk serves as a stairway to the outer, open verandah, where the families congregate, dry their washing or lay out their fish, spices, fruit, nuts and vegetables. On the inner, closed verandah are the communal 'lounges', kept for recreation and ceremonies.

Off to the side behind partitions, family dwellings consist of bedrooms and kitchens. An attic under the roof is used for storing grain or rice. The attic sometimes doubles as a weaving room.

Modern times have brought running tap-water, electricity generators, cooking stoves, radio and television. However, people also keep their traditions, wearing sarongs and proudly bearing hornbill tattoos on their throat and arms. Hanging from pillars and rafters are the ancestral head-hunting trophies – believed to give the clan strength and good fortune.

Melanau tall house, Sarawak Cultural Village *(see page 109)*

(see page 109)

early and involve a two- to five-hour road journey to the river and then a one-hour cruise by longboat. Tour operators usually have exclusive arrangements with particular longhouses.

The format of a visit varies, but it may include cultural performances soon after arrival for day-trippers or at the day's end as evening entertainment for those staying longer. The standard tour is an initial orientation to the longhouse, highlighting the *bilik* (apartments) as distinct from the *ruai* (communal areas). Tour groups are often greeted with *tuak*, a sweet wine made from glutinous rice, and a welcome dance. The musical and cultural performance includes a *ngajat*, a traditional Iban dance. Demonstrations of the blowpipe and cockfighting are also likely to be on the agenda.

Before you leave, your tour guide will remind you to make sure that you have gifts – preferably nutritious food, clothes or children's books – which can be bought during one of the bus stopovers on the way. Sweets and junk food are inappropriate. Malaysian tourism authorities are also able to offer advice on reputable tour operators in Kuching who organise visits on a small scale so as not to offend tribal customs.

Tours are available to **Iban** longhouses around Kuching, and **Bidayuh** longhouses in the hill regions. Visits to Iban communities are possible along the **Skrang** and **Batang Ai rivers**. To the east of Kuching you can visit the **Kenyah** and **Kayan** tribes. Excursions are organised either via Miri from Kuala Baram along the majestic **Baram River**, or via Sibu, from Kapit or Belaga, up the **Rejang River**. The Rejang is considered Malaysia's greatest river at some 560km (350 miles) long; a journey along it is considered one of the world's last great travel adventures. The approach to Belaga entails a passage through the Rejang's **Pelagus Rapids**. There are seven in all: *Bidai* (big mat), *Nabau* (python), *Lunggak* (dagger), *Pantu* (sago), *Sukat* (measure), *Mawang* (fruit) and, most ominously, *Rapoh* (tomb).

Niah National Park

At **Niah Caves** visitors can see the earliest traces of *Homo sapiens* in Malaysia; they lived in the area up to 40,000 years ago. Later the caves were used as burial grounds, and they are now the hunting-ground of collectors of birds' nests located on the cave roofs. The caves and surrounding 3,149-hectare (7,775-acre) park are 480km (300 miles) up the coast from Kuching, hidden within the forests around Miri.

Adventurer A. Hart Everett came across the caves in the 1870s, but it was not until 1958 that local explorer and Sarawak Museum curator Tom Harrisson made the important discovery of a human skull dating back some 37,000 years, together with 1,200-year-old red hematite rock paintings. The fragments of the Deep Skull (so-called because it was found deep within an ancient pile of bat guano), together with tools, earthenware pots, jars and later bronze jewellery found nearby are on display in the Kuching Museum.

Inside Niah Caves

The park, near the town of Batu Niah, is midway between
Bintulu and **Miri**, the latter a boomcity known for its oil exploration. The caves are accessible by road from either settlement, taking at least two hours from Miri and three hours
from Bintulu. The park's headquarters is at **Pengkalan Batu**,
and you will need to obtain a permit either here or in Miri.
From here, you cross the Sungei Niah (or Niah River) by
sampan, then follow the 3km (2-mile) boardwalk to the
caves. For the cave tour, be sure to take a powerful flashlight,
sturdy walking shoes with a good grip and a change of
clothes – the heat and humidity are quite intense.

First seen is the **Traders Cave**, so-called because of its
role as a meeting place for bird's nest gatherers and merchants. The main or **Great Cave** is a hollow 400m
(1,312ft) up in the sandstone Subis Plateau. Besides giant
crickets and scorpions (from which the extension of the
boardwalk through the cave keeps you safe), the cave is

home to millions of bats and swiftlets. The Deep Skull and other relics were discovered here.

The bats' daily droppings furnish one tonne of highly valued guano fertiliser. But more lucrative than the guano are the swiftlets' edible nests – used to make bird's-nest soup – for which Chinese merchants are prepared to pay hundreds of dollars per kilo (about 100 nests), reselling them for thousands. Park authorities are increasingly concerned about the impact of the on-going harvest on the swiftlets' survival. The rush of nesting swiftlets flying into the cave at the day's end, while nocturnal bats rush past into the evening sky, is a spectacular sight.

The boardwalk continues through the Great Cave down to the **Painted Cave**, also accessible without a guide. Discovered in 1958 along with the Deep Skull, its wall-paintings representing red stick-figures of spread-eagle dancers were executed in a mixture of betel juice and lime around AD700. This cave was probably also used as a burial chamber.

Bird's-Nest Soup

Descendants of the nomadic Penan people who rediscovered the Niah Caves' bird's-nest riches in the 19th century divide up the cave into jealously guarded 'stakes', handed down from father to son. To scrape the nests from the cave ceiling, the Penan climb more than 60m (200ft) up a series of swaying bamboo poles tied together, or through narrow 'chimneys' inside the rock. As the old song says, 'A lotta men did and a lotta men died' – nobody knows how many.

White-bellied swiftlets are responsible for the high-priced nests, made from pure saliva rendered particularly glutinous by a diet of algae. An inferior product is furnished by 'black-nest' swiftlets who mix feathers in with the saliva. While not for everyone, Chinese diners insist that the viscous, translucent soup is delicious.

Nearby are several forest trails, with the **Bukit Kasut** and the **Madu trails** both clearly marked. Look out for long-tailed macaques, together with a range of birdlife such as bulbuls, tailor birds, crested wood partridges, trogons and hornbills.

Gunung Mulu National Park

Among the largest limestone cave systems in the world, the Unesco World Heritage Site of **Gunung Mulu National Park** (53,000 hectares/130,600 acres) is one of Sarawak's most important attractions. The cave system of 150km (94 miles) was first explored between 1976 and 1984 and requires a minimum two-day/one-night stay to be fully appreciated. The trip is demanding, and you need to be in good shape, especially if you are looking to undertake the climb to the limestone-sculpted pinnacles on Gunung Api (Fire Mountain).

A 35-minute flight from **Miri** arrives at the airport near the park's headquarters. The alternative (by land and boat) also starts from Miri and is a four-stage trip. First, you travel by bus or taxi to Kuala Baram, at the mouth of the Batang Baram. From here, you take an express boat to **Marudi** before meeting up with the noon boat to **Long Terawan**, followed by a third longboat along the Sungei Tutoh and Sungei Melinau to the park's headquarters. This is the only alternative to the air trip and requires almost a full day of travel by bus and boat. The flight from Miri over rainforest in a small aircraft is

Mulu's caves

With permits, experienced cavers can explore Mulu's less accessible caves and wade chest-deep through underground streams. The best guides will provide miner's helmets with built-in lamps to explore the pitch-black caves. Your own equipment should include very strong shoes made of rubber rather than leather, lots of socks, tough old clothes, a pair of gloves and a light sleeping bag.

The spectacular pinnacles on Mount Api

considered the best way to begin your stay at Mulu and is also recommended for the return journey.

There are four main 'show caves' at Mulu – Deer, Lang's, Clearwater and Wind – as well as countless other 'wild caves', which are either too dangerous or too ecologically fragile to visit without special permits and qualified guides.

To give you an idea of the vast scale of the caverns, **Sarawak Chamber**, reputed to be the largest cave in the world, is said to be capable of holding 40 jumbo jets. Tours began in 1998, but entry is usually restricted to seasoned cavers. If you wish to see this spectacular chamber, ask for details well in advance when making your booking.

Nearest to the park's headquarters are the **Deer Cave** and Lang's Cave. The Deer Cave, with an enormous entrance and a passage 2km (1 mile) long and up to 220m (720ft) high, was once a shelter for deer. It is uncertain whether it was also used as a human burial ground, as other caves in the system

Mulu's Deer Cave

were. Like many other large, open caves, it is home to millions of bats, which fly out in a cloud at dusk in search of food. Noteworthy is 'Adam and Eve's shower', a cascade of water falling 120m (393ft) from the cave's ceiling. Deep within the cave – reached after about an hour's walking – is a hidden green valley known as the **Garden of Eden**.

Lang's Cave, nearby, was once inhabited by wild boars, and, although smaller, it has a variety of stalactites and stalagmites and spectacular rock curtains.

Both the **Clearwater** and **Wind Caves** are reached by longboat from park headquarters. The Clearwater Cave's passage extends for 50km (31 miles). After passing the moss-covered stalactites near the entrance, you'll need a good flashlight in order to see the limestone formations. Wind Cave is accessible to hardy cavers from near the Clearwater Cave, but other visitors must make their entry from the riverbank.

Exploring the **Pinnacles**, 900m (2,950ft) up the side of Mount Api, will add extra days to the tour, but there are few sights to match these gigantic stone needles thrusting like petrified hooded ghosts above the dark-green canopy of the forest. Extra time, too, is required if you wish to attempt the climb up **Mount Mulu** (2,376m/7,793ft), whose summit was successfully reached by Lord Shackleton in 1932 after earlier known attempts in the 19th century had failed. The ascent of Mount Mulu alone can take up to five days, although experienced climbers have made the journey in less than two.

The richness of the park's flora and fauna has been the topic of many scientific studies, revealing 1,500 species of flowering plant, 4,000 varieties of fungus, 75 species of mammal, 262 species of bird, 50 species of reptile and 281 species of butterfly. Bird-life includes stork-billed kingfishers along rivers and strawheaded bulbuls in the forests.

Sabah

Covering the northern tip of Borneo, Sabah lies just clear of the cyclones that regularly sweep down across the Philippines, and so has been dubbed by generations of sailors the 'Land Below the Winds'. Its capital, Kota Kinabalu – popularly known as KK – looks over the South China Sea, with the Sulu to the northeast and the Sulawesi Seas to the south.

KK lies in the shadow of the Crocker Mountain Range, home of Mount Kinabalu, one of Southeast Asia's tallest mountains at 4,101m (13,455ft). The Kinabalu National Park is just one of several protected regions in the state.

The capital also serves as a gateway for visits to an offshore national park of coral islands. On the east coast, Sandakan provides a base for visiting the Turtle Islands, the famous orang-utans of Sepilok and the Kinabatangan River. Visitors can choose from fishing, snorkelling, deep-sea diving, leisurely coral cruises in the beautiful waters surrounding Sabah, or just exploring KK's markets.

Kota Kinabalu

Known as Jesselton (after Sir Charles Jessel, chairman of the North Borneo Chartered Co.) until World War II, **Kota Kinabalu** was renamed Api (Fire) by the occupying Japanese. Today's KK was rebuilt from the ashes of the war after Allied bombing razed the city during the Japanese occupation. KK is at present a prosperous and busy seaport, with a growing manufacturing base and a population of 450,000. Rebuilt in a modern style, it is blessed with a beautiful natural setting: tree-clad coral islands off the coast and the dramatic backdrop of Mount Kinabalu to the west. The city is generally used as a base for visiting the surrounding national parks. You'll find a **tourist information office** (a former post office) on Jalan Gaya.

The large, golden dome of the **State Mosque**, at the corner of Jalan Tunku Abdul Rahman and Jalan Penampang, can be seen as you come into town from the airport. Nearby is the **Sabah State Museum** or Jalan Museum (Sat–Thur). The museum is styled along the lines of Murut and Rungus longhouses, and set in grounds where you will also find a number of steam engines. Its historic photographic collection provides a chance to see the township as it was before the devastation of war.

White-water rafting

Next door is the **Science and Technology Centre** and an **Art Gallery**. Across from the museum is an **Ethnobotanic Garden**, offering the chance to see a range of tropical plants.

One block east of Jalan Gaya is the **Atkinson Clock Tower**, built in 1905. Along with the tourist information office, it is one of the few prewar structures still standing.

Walk up the hill to enjoy the view from the **Signal Hill Observatory**. One of the most popular markets in town is the **Jalan Gaya Street Market**, held every Sunday morning. At the waterfront can be found the **Filipino Market**, near the general and fish markets.

On the north side of town is the gleaming **Sabah Foundation** building, a 30-storey landmark. Construction of the tower was financed by timber royalties to the state, after the foundation, devoted to state educational projects, was established in 1966. Views from the @mosphere revolving restaurant, located at the top, are stunning. Plan to be here at sunset to appreciate the best views of KK.

The Coral Islands

Just a brief boat ride from KK are the five islands of the **Tunku Abdul Rahman Park**, which was created in 1974. Boats can be rented at the waterfront, near the Hyatt Hotel, for either a group or individual tour to the islands. All five islands lie within an 8km (5-mile) radius and provide first-class beaches and superb opportunities for swimming and snorkelling, and there are boardwalk trails into the islands' forested interiors.

Pulau Gaya is the largest of the coral islands. The park headquarters here can give you information about the flora and fauna, both underwater and in the forest. The sandy **Police Beach** on the north shore is good for swimming and exploring marine life among the coral reefs. On the boardwalk trail across a mangrove-swamp forest, look out for monkeys, bearded pigs and pied hornbills.

Some of the best nature trails are on neighbouring **Pulau Sapi**, a 10-hectare (25-acre) islet off the northwestern coast of Pulau Gaya. South of Sapi is **Pulau Manukan**, the most developed of the islands, with hilltop and beach-side chalets, a restaurant, swimming pool, and tennis and squash courts. Tiny **Pulau Mamutik**, covering just 6 hectares (15 acres) and

Malaysia is known for its great diversity of coral species

largely unspoiled, with plenty of reefs at its northeastern end, is very popular with divers and snorkellers. The most remote and least developed island, with the park's finest coral reefs and abundant marine life, **Pulau Sulug** offers a more tranquil and deserted atmosphere.

Around Kota Kinabalu

From the bus station near Jalan Tun Razak, inexpensive journeys can be made to locations not far from the city. Visit one of the many *tamu* (village markets) held on different days of the week – ask at Kota Kinabalu's tourist information office. The best are at **Tuaran** 33km (20 miles) from KK, and further north at Kota Belud, where one finds the **Mengkabong** and **Penambawan** Bajau villages.

At Donggongon in the village of Kuai, 10km (6 miles) south of KK on Penampang River, is the Kampung Monsopiad. It was built to commemorate the legendary warrior Monsopiad, whose forte was beheading his enemies. Forty-two of his 'trophies' are on show at the **Cultural Village**.

To view the nearby tropical forests, ride on the railway to **Beaufort**, and another 40km (25 miles) northwest to the town of **Tenom**, with its **Agricultural Research Station**. Although the train begins its journey at Tanjung Aru, you can save time by taking a taxi to Beaufort and then another from Tenom back to Kota Kinabalu. At Beaufort, Chinese shophouses stand on stilts next to the Padas River. The **North Borneo Railway**, an old-fashioned steam locomotive, runs to Papar a few times a week.

South from KK, heading towards the Crocker Mountain Range, is the **Rafflesia Centre**. This is dedicated to the world's largest flower, the rafflesia, of which there are 14 varieties.

Kinabalu Park

The refreshing temperatures and spectacular scenery make a journey to **Kinabalu Park**, a Unesco World Heritage Site, more than worthwhile. Even if you avoid the vigorous climb to the mountain's summit, the scenery, plants and wildlife close to the park's headquarters are rewarding. Looming huge and dark in the light of dawn, the peak is revealed in its full splendour, but morning clouds often sweep upwards again to shroud it in mist.

At 4,101m (13,455ft), **Mount Kinabalu** is one of the highest peaks between the Himalayas and New Guinea. Its name means 'sacred home of the dead' to the Kadazan who live on its lower slopes. The park can be reached by road 90km (56 miles) from Kota Kinubalu. There is a special bus service from KK, but arrive early, as it departs once full. The trip to the park headquarters takes at least two hours, though only one and a half hours on return. There are also regular buses plying the highway between KK and Sandakan. The journey from Kota Kinabalu to the park and the climb up into the Crocker Range takes you through Malaysia's varieties of forest and landscape, from lowland dipterocarp forest to sub-alpine meadow.

The park covers 754 sq km (291 sq miles), with temperatures far cooler than on the coast. They ease to a gentle 20°C (68°F) at park headquarters and can drop to freezing point at the lodge where climbers spend the night prior to their assault on the summit, so warm clothing is a must, as well as rainproof clothing for those climbing the mountain *(see page 159)*.

To climb the summit, book at the **Sabah Parks Headquarters** in Kota Kinabalu well in advance, especially in April, July, August and December. The climb takes two days, with an overnight stay halfway up. Foreigners pay more than locals. The park has a good restaurant and accommodation ranging from chalets to simple hostels. At the park's headquarters arrangements are made for mountain guides, porters and transport to the station where the climb begins. Trail maps are available for those who want to set out on their own (but be careful, as some trails are not as well marked as others). Hardy souls may like to swim in the cool Liwago River nearby. A small **Mountain Garden** provides a good introduction to the plant life you will find in Kinabalu's forest.

The pride of the mountain's plant life is its 1,200 different orchids, found up to an altitude of 3,800m (12,464ft). Ferns are also present in their hundreds. Rhododendron-lovers may find 25 different varieties, together with 60 types of oak and chestnuts. But the most fascinating flora remain the pink-speckled, carnivorous pitcher plants *(see below)*.

The Pitcher Plant

The pitcher plant consists of a bowl often shaped like a miniature tuba with a curved lid sticking upright when open. Why do insects fall in? Those that go for the nectar under the pitcher lid get away safely. Others going for the nectar glands under the pitcher's rim fall into a digestive liquid mixture of rainwater and enzymes. Unable to climb back up the sticky, scaly interior, they drown and are slowly digested. Cashing in on the activity around these plants, some spiders spin webs across the inside of the pitcher's mouth and catch the falling insects.

The giant of the species is the *Nepenthes rajah*, with one pitcher measuring a record 46cm (18in) and holding 4 litres (7 pints) of water. They have been found digesting frogs and even rats.

Splendid Mount Kinabalu

Many of the local forest's 100 mammals are difficult to spot; the few orang-utans, for instance, are practically invisible, but you can at least hear the gibbons whooping. Besides the usual sambar and mousedeer, bearded pigs and clouded leopards, there are 28 species of squirrel as well as the slow loris and the western tarsier. Kinabalu also has some 326 species of birds, including the scarlet sunbird, whitehead's spider-hunter, grey drongo, crested serpent eagle and white-rumped shama.

Each year a marathon race – or 'Climbathon' – is held on the mountain. The record is presently held by a British man, Ian Holmes, who ran to the summit in just 2 hours, 42.07 seconds. For ordinary mortals, meals and bedding are provided at the mountain lodges for the overnight stop. Rates differ between weekdays and weekends. Armed with warm and rainproof clothing, flashlight, and bananas and chocolate for energy, you make an early morning start. After a stretch of road, the climb proper begins at **Timpohon Gate**. As you

The unmistakable Donkey's Ears

climb, you will notice the change from bamboo groves to oaks (the forest here has 40 different varieties), myrtle, laurel and moss-covered pines. The trees become more gnarled and stunted as you approach the barren granite plateau at the summit.

The first shelter at **Carson's Falls** is at 1,951m (6,400ft). The best chance to see pitcher plants on the trail is at the **Second Shelter** on the trail at 2,134m (7,000ft), but remember, no picking. You make your overnight stop at the **Laban Rata Rest-house**, or the **Panar Laban Hut**, **Waras Hut**, or **Gunting Lagadan** at 3,353m (11,000ft). *Panar Laban* means Place of Sacrifice: here seven white chickens and seven eggs are offered each year by Kadazan climbers to the spirits of the sacred mountain.

To get to the summit at sunrise, you must get up at about 2am and make your way up across a barren granite plateau. The **Sayat Sayat Huts**, 3,811m (12,500ft), are the last shelters before the summit. Directly to the north are the **Donkey's Ears** rocks, and behind them the **Ugly Sisters**, as you make your way west to **Low's Peak** (4,101m/13,455ft), the highest of the mountain's nine peaks. The view from the Crocker Range and towards the Philippines is staggering. But one cannot stay long, as the summit soon becomes enveloped in mid-morning mists, making the descent treacherous for even experienced climbers.

Poring Hot Springs

The **Poring Hot Springs**, 37km (23 miles) from the park head-quarters, offer great relief after the tough climb down the mountain. The springs, with their soothing sulphur baths, were developed by the Japanese during World War II. Cool off at the **Langanan Waterfall** along one of trails, or at the **Kepungit Waterfall**, a site rich in butterflies and bat-filled caves. Near-by are groves of bamboo (*poring* means bamboo in Kadazan), a canopy walk, lodgings in chalets and hostels and a campsite.

Sandakan

Stretched along a narrow strip of land between steep hills and the Sulu Sea, **Sandakan** is the gateway to the Turtle Islands Park, the Gomtanong Caves and the Sepilok Orang-Utan Sanctuary. Once the capital of British North Borneo, modern Sandakan, like Kota Kinabalu, was devastated during World War II, leaving little evidence of the former township.

The lively **Waterfront Market** is a good starting point for visitors. Sandakan's oldest temple, built in the 1880s, is dedicated to the **Goddess of Mercy**, although modernisation has detracted from its character. The ornate **Puu Jih Shih Buddhist Temple**, ablaze with dragons and gilded Buddhas, stands on the hilltop above Tanah Merah, south of Sandakan town.

You can also tour the home of **Agnes Keith**, an American writer whose life in Sandakan from 1932–54, including experiences in a prisoner-of-war camp, was documented in three novels, including *Land Below the Wind*. Her pre-war home was destroyed but reconstructed and is now a museum. Next door is the superb English Tea House Restaurant.

Other links to the war include the **Australian Memorial** on the site of the former prisoner-of-war camp in Taman Rimba, off Labuk Road. It commemorates the Allied soldiers who died during the Japanese occupation and serves as a remembrance of the Death March by 2,400 mostly Australian soldiers – of whom just six survived – from the camp to Ranau in September 1944. There is also a small Japanese graveyard in the corner of the old cemetery on the hills overlooking the town.

The Lower Kinabatangan River Basin

The Kinabatangan Basin, 80km (50 miles) southwest of Sandakan, offers a good chance to catch sight of a range of wildlife, especially Bornean pygmy elephants, hornbills, monitor lizards, macaques and orang-utans, not to mention the elusive proboscis monkey. The Kinabatangan is a rewarding river for wildlife fans, with trips organised by Sandakan tour operators.

Another access point to the wilds of Sabah is through the **Danum Valley Conservation Area**. The valley is 80km (50 miles) inland from Lahad Datu on Sabah's east coast. Here are a range of walking trails through the protected forests, home to the western tarsier, orang-utan, leopard cat, deer, Malayan sun bear, the very rare Sumatran rhinoceros, smooth otter and 275 species of birdlife. Visitors can stay in the Borneo Rainforest Lodge and visit the wilderness area of the Maliau Basin.

The Sepilok Orang-Utan Sanctuary

A 30-minute drive west of Sandakan, this nature reserve provides a rehabilitation centre for young orang-utans, previously

Orang-Utans

In Malay, orang-utan means 'forest person' – an appropriate mark of respect for the mammal biologically closest to man. These intelligent, russet-coloured apes live in the swamp forests of Sabah and Sarawak. They are very individualistic nomads, meeting occasionally to share a fruit supper before going their own way. Some visitors to Sepilok confuse them with the similarly coloured red-leaf monkeys – but unlike monkeys, orang-utans have no tails.

held in captivity. This prepares them to live alone in the
forest. Boardwalk trails take
visitors to the feeding areas.

These highly theatrical apes
exist at three levels in Sepilok's: tame, entirely in the
care of zoologists; semi-tame,
living within reach of the
sanctuary's feeding points;
and wild, having moved off to
remote parts of the forest
away from their prying
human cousins. Many of the
orang-utans are as curious as
the visitors. They have flashy

See orang-utans at Sepilok

tastes, preferring to snatch at bright objects rather than dull
ones. They also have a good sense of parody. Watching someone put up an umbrella in the rain, they will immediately mimic
this, using leaves and twigs. They also show a weary disdain
for the antics of photographers leaping around them.

Optimistic figures put the numbers of orang-utans at between 10,000 and 20,000 in Sabah. While still free from
being listed as endangered, fears nevertheless remain that
unchecked forest clearing will sharply reduce their numbers.

Turtle Islands Park

All year round, green and hawksbill turtles gather to lay their
eggs on the island beaches north of Sandakan Bay. The park
is 40km (25 miles) from Sandakan and comprises three islands – **Pulau Selingaan**, **Pulau Bakkungan** and **Pulau
Gulisaan** – covering 1,740 hectares (4,295 acres). At Pulau
Selingaan there are several furnished chalets where up to 20
visitors can stay overnight and maintain their night-long vigil.

WHAT TO DO

Sightseeing is, of course, only a part of your visit to Malaysia. You will probably want to take time to shop for traditional arts and crafts in Kuching, check out the night markets of Kuala Lumpur, or drop by a few Chinese antiques shops in Penang. Those who wish to can have quite an active holiday just sampling the local shopping scene. Malaysia offers a showcase of festivals of events and festivities throughout the year as well.

SHOPPING

An excellent variety of goods is available throughout Malaysia. Large department stores and malls are to be found in most major cities, with night markets adding colour, while antiques shops brim with traditional handicrafts and Chinese antiques. Batik fabric designs, silver- and pewter-ware and silk brocaded *songket* cloth are popular items.

The night markets often offer many fresh food items and clothing that is very competitively priced. In Sabah, you may even be able to buy a buffalo, though shipping is not included in the purchase price. Away from the major department stores bargaining is expected; but make sure on more expensive items that you have a good idea of retail prices before you begin.

Malaysia's tax havens are Pulau Langkawi and Labuan. Duty-free areas are also found at Rantau Panjang and Pengkalan Kubur, both in Kelantan; Padang Besar and Bukit Kayu Hitam in Kedah; and Pulau Tioman (Tioman Island) in Pahang. Duty-free shops can also be found at all international airports.

Top-spinning or *gasing* is a popular east coast sport

What to Buy

Most major towns have **handicraft stores** like KL's Craft Complex on Jalan Conlay, which act as a showcase for products from all over the peninsula and East Malaysia. KL's Central Market gives you a wider selection. As far as quality is concerned, some of the best traditional products are to be found in the **museum shops** in Kuala Lumpur, Melaka, Kuching and Kota Kinabalu. The selection is more comprehensive in the markets and shops of Kelantan, Terengganu, Sarawak and Sabah. In Kota Bharu or Kuala Terengganu, take a guided *kampung* tour to see the artisans at work – you'll often find that you can get their products at a better price than in town.

Batik: Bright and enticing, these colourfully patterned fabrics are today both hand- and factory-made in Kelantan and Terengganu, but had their origins in the Malay kingdoms of

Songket, the favoured cloth for royal occasions

Java more than 1,000 years ago. The technique remains the same, although it was adopted on the peninsula only in the 20th century. A design of melted wax is applied to cotton or silk, using a metal stencil. The fabric is then dipped in cool vegetable or synthetic dye, which colours the cloth around the wax pattern. The piece is then dipped in hot water to remove the wax, leaving a lighter design behind. The process may be repeated for multiple colouring. Tradi-

A Chinese painter in KL's Central Market

tionally, certain designs were reserved for royalty, but today elegant geometric or exuberant, stylised floral patterns are available to all. You can either purchase the cloth and have it tailored back home or buy a sarong – useful at the beach over a bikini. Other items include hats, scarves, ties, purses, shirts and wall-hangings. Do note that the quality of batik can vary greatly.

Kain Songket: *Kain Songket* (silk brocade) is a speciality of Terengganu. On a hardwood frame, silver and gold threads are woven into fine silk, usually of emerald green, dark red, purple, or royal blue. Besides geometric and floral patterns, you will also find handsome fan and dagger motifs. *Songket* was originally reserved for royalty, but is today also used for bridal dresses, ceremonial robes, cushion-covers and handbags.

Silverwork and pewter: The silversmith's centuries-old skills, originally developed at the court of Perak, are continued

A selection of Malaysian crafts

today in rural Kelantan. As Islam prohibits the representation of human or animal figures, the work done here is the happy result of imposing much simpler patterns than the often elaborate silverware across the border in Thailand. The work remains exquisite despite this perceived limitation. Besides earrings, brooches, necklaces and bracelets, you will find plaques and filigree jewellery, perfume bottles, snuff boxes (originally designed for betel nuts), belt buckles, caskets, lacquered trays and magnificent bowls.

Pewter-work, in the form of goblets, clocks, tankards, wine carafes, trays and salt- and pepper-shakers, is a luxury side-product of the tin industry. It is actually 95 percent tin, hardened with a 5 percent alloy of antimony and copper. The major names to look out for are Royal Selangor and Tumasek Pewter, both available throughout the country. Royal Selangor is on sale in KL at several major hotels as well as department stores. It is also made and sold in Singapore. The Tumasek Pewter factory is on Jalan Kuang Bulan in Taman Kepong, KL.

Other craftwork: One of the most attractive products of the traditional arts is the highly decorative **puppet** used in the *wayang kulit* shadow theatre *(see page 138)*. The demons, clowns and kings that you can watch being made in a Kelantan rural workshop can make splendid ornaments.

More practical but quite decorative are bamboo and rattan **baskets** and **mats** woven from nipa palm leaves.

In **Kuching** look for Iban *pua kumbu* (hand-woven **blankets**), wooden hornbill carvings used in rituals, and silver jewellery, woven Bidayuh baskets, Orang Ulu beadwork and woodcarving, and Penan blowpipes and mats. Most antiques and curio shops are around the Main Bazaar just beside the Waterfront, with a few in the Padungan area.

An authentic **blowpipe** is one of the most accomplished pieces of indigenous craftwork in all of Malaysia. Really good ones are now increasingly rare and quite expensive, and their length, 2m (over 6ft), makes them difficult to carry around. Failing a real hardwood blowpipe, you can buy the handsome quiver of stout, rattan-bound bamboo with the poison darts (minus the poison), both authentic, and a shorter pipe of bamboo that does a perfectly serviceable job of blowing darts into your cork dartboard at home.

Straight and Narrow Blowpipes

Kayan, Kenyah and nomadic Penan hunters make the best *sumpitan* (blowpipes) from coveted Sarawak straight-grained hardwood. From the felled tree, they cut a piece about 2.5m (8ft) long and shave it with an adze to a cylindrical form about 10cm (4in) in diameter. This straight but rough pole is lashed firmly to a series of supports so as to stand perfectly upright. Its upper end projects above a platform where an artisan – with a chisel-pointed iron rod for a drill – slowly and meticulously bores a dead straight hole down through the pole. The weapon's bore must be as clean and polished as that of a rifle barrel for the dart to pass through unimpeded. Its shaft is shaved, rounded and smoothed to produce a finished blowpipe of about 2½cm (1in) in diameter.

The pipe often comes with a sharp spear point at its non-blowing end to finish off larger prey that would only have been stunned by the poison in the dart, such as deer, wild pig or, perhaps, in the old days, humans. The poison is made from the sap of the ipoh tree.

Point of etiquette

Avoid pointing with your fingers, which in Malay culture is considered rude. It is better to extend the flat of your hand in the direction you wish to indicate.

Sarawak **pottery** is ochre-coloured with bold geometric designs. Sayong pottery, from Perak, has a glossy black colour. There is even pottery from Johor, decorated with batik and gold thread, giving it a distinctive look.

Antiques: Melaka's Baba Nyonya Chinese quarter *(see page 63)* is a great place to hunt and bargain for old porcelain imported from southern China, antique silver or jade bracelets, and, if you can find a way of shipping it home, a piece of furniture from the colonial days. Penang is also popular for antiques-lovers along Jalan Pintal Tali (Rope Walk), offering porcelain-ware, chains, coins, old glass, ceiling lamps and antique clocks. Occasionally treasures can be unearthed – notably old Chinese theatrical costumes and fake jewellery – as you rummage among the piles of junk in George Town's famous flea market at Lorong Kulit.

Discount and duty-free goods: You can get good deals on **watches**, **jewellery**, major brand **sports clothes** and **jeans** in the **street markets** of Kuala Lumpur – especially around Chinatown's Jalan Petaling – and of George Town along Jalan Penang, Lebuh Campbell and Lebuh Chulia. Bargaining here is almost compulsory. The fakes are best distinguished from the genuine articles by how low a price the vendor will accept. If you find you are acquiring an incredible bargain, start asking yourself whether that is what you want to pay for a piece of counterfeit merchandise, albeit a brilliant one.

There are many excellent and **modern shopping centres** in KL on and around Jalan Bukit Bintang, near the bigger international hotels. These include Lot 10, the Pavilion, KLCC and Starhill Gallery.

ENTERTAINMENT

Nightlife

To cater to Western tastes, the major cities – KL, George Town, Melaka, Johor Bahru, Kuantan, Kuching and Kota Kinabalu – and the beach resorts have nightclubs and cocktail lounges with live music. The jazz and popular music scene is mostly dominated by Filipino performers of very high calibre. The singers deliver stunning carbon-copy renditions of current and past hits, while the musicians are quite brilliant in their set pieces or improvisations.

Traditional Dance and Theatre

Malaysia's traditional entertainment is more often than not a daytime affair. Tourist information offices in Kota Bharu and Kuala Terengganu can inform you about times and reserva-

Dancers from the annual 'Colours of Malaysia' celebrations

Festival fun

Malaysians love celebrating, and with so many different religions – Islam, Hinduism, Buddhism, Christianity and aboriginal animism – they give themselves plenty of opportunities. They often join in each other's festivities, Muslims inviting Chinese friends to their Hari Raya feasts to end the fast of Ramadan, and members of all the communities turning up for Melaka's Christian processions at Easter.

tions. This information can also be found at the Malaysia Tourism Office in KL.

Mak Yong dance drama: This elegant art form evolved over 400 years ago in the Malay state of Pattani, now part of southern Thailand, and today is performed across the border in Kelantan. It consists of a play on one of a dozen set romantic themes, accompanied by dance, operatic singing and knockabout comic routines. The latter is accomplished by the men, while all the other performers are beautifully costumed women. The orchestra of *rebab* (bowed fiddle), *tawak-tawk* (gongs) and *gendang* (double-headed drums) plays music with a distinctly Middle Eastern flavour.

Wayang Kulit shadow theatre: The most popular form of shadow theatre is known as *Wayang Siam*. It is of Malay rather than Siamese origin, drawing on themes from the Hindu epic *Ramayana*. It dates back more than 1,000 years to when Indian merchants first brought their Hindu culture to the peninsula. The stories surrounding Prince Rama and his wife Sita involve ogres, demon-kings and monkey warriors, all represented on stage by puppets. With its customary cheerfulness, Malay culture has added a comic element absent from the high drama of the original.

The small timber and bamboo theatre is mounted on stilts, and the puppets are seen as sharply etched shadows cast on a white cotton screen by a lamp hanging from the roof of the theatre. One *dalang* (puppeteer), accompanied by a band of musicians playing oboes, drums, gongs and cymbals, acts out all the parts and produces all the different voices. He peeps from behind the screen to assess the age and sophistication of his audience and varies the play accordingly. Originally, all the brightly coloured puppets were made from cow-, buffalo-, or goat-hides, but today the minor characters are turned out in plastic and celluloid. The bright colours are said to vary the intensity of the shadows and help differentiate the characters.

SPORTS

Water Sports

Most large hotels and resorts have their own **swimming pools**, which are a necessity in the hot climate. The coolest and most exhilarating swim is to be had in the natural pools

Fishing from a *sampan*

of the waterfalls of Taman Negara and Mount Kinabalu national parks. But if you prefer good sandy **beaches**, head for the east coast. The beaches of Kelantan and Terengganu, especially the near-deserted Rantau Abang, and further south at Johor's Desaru, haven't yet suffered as much from industrialisation as those on the west coast. But Tioman Island has some of the east coast's best beaches, particularly if you like secluded coves. On the west coast, your best bets are the resorts on Penang, Pangkor or Langkawi islands. In Sarawak, the best beaches are northwest of Kuching, at Damai, Santubong or Bako National Park; in Sabah, either at Kota Kinabalu's offshore islands of the Tunku Abdul Rahman Park or up at Kudat on Borneo's northernmost tip; over on Sabah's east coast try the islands off Sandakan Bay.

Scuba diving among barracuda

The resorts offer excellent amenities for all types of water sports: **snorkelling**, **scuba diving**, **windsurfing**, **sailing** and **water-skiing**. Scuba divers should remember that the coral and other marine life are protected species and are not to be touched or damaged.

Other Sports

The British have left their mark; the country has more than 250 golf courses, with a choice of 9-, 18-, 27- and 54-holes. When the local course is private, as at the

Royal Perak Golf Club in Ipoh, your hotel may be able to get you temporary membership if you are a member of a golf club back home. Take your card along just in case. The most refreshing courses are in the cooler hill stations, notably Cameron Highlands and Fraser's Hill. The best of the courses is at Saujana Golf and Country Club near KL, but there are pleasant 18-hole courses on Langkawi Island as well. Golfers say that the best resort course is the Bukit Jambul Golf Club in Penang.

The national sport, **badminton**, is played wherever a net, real or makeshift, can be set up for players to thwack the shuttlecock across to each other. Many resort hotels provide proper courts.

Tennis facilities are also widely available, but the climate makes it a sport best reserved for early morning, or evenings, when the courts are floodlit. **Squash** has become a popular racket game and facilities are widely available.

Freshwater **fishing** is a delight in the mountain streams of Taman Negara and Kinabalu parks or on Lakes Chini and Kenyir. Off the east coast, you could try **deep-sea fishing** for barracuda or shark. In all cases, enquire first at tourist information offices about the necessary fishing permits. **Hunting** licences are so restricted that it is scarcely worth the trouble for ordinary tourists.

Traditional Malay Sports

Like the arts and crafts, ancient Malay sports and pastimes are practised almost exclusively on the east coast, though you may also see demonstrations elsewhere at cultural centres in KL or Sarawak. The best time to see them is in the weeks following the rice harvest and during the special festivals that stage statewide contests (see page 143).

Kelantan and Terengganu preserve a centuries-old tradition of **flying ornamental kites** measuring 2m (6ft 6ins) across and the same from head to tail. In *kampung* workshops you can watch fantastic birds and butterflies being made of paper (and increasingly of plastic, too) drawn over strong, flexible bamboo frames. Village contests judge competitors on their most spectacular flying skills – height, dexterity and the humming sound produced by the wind through the kite-head.

Like kite flying, **top-spinning** is no mere child's game. Adults can keep a top in motion for over 50 minutes. The top looks somewhat like a discus, made of hardwood with a steel knob or spike in the centre and a lead rim. The standard size is about 23cm (9in) in diameter. It takes some six weeks to complete the construction of what is considered to be a precision instrument. Villages stage team games with the objective of keeping a top spinning for the longest time. Another derivative of the game, using a different kind of top, has for its objective knocking the opponent's top out of the spinning area.

Sepak Takraw is a kind of volleyball played with a ball made of rattan, which the players can hit with every part of their body except hands and forearms. One team has to get over the net to the other team, without being in contact with the ball more than three times on their side of the court. A three-man team scores points each time the ball hits the ground on the opponent's court or if the ball is hit out of the court.

Lion dance in Kuala Lumpur

The Malay martial art **silat** came from Sumatra some 400 years ago. It is performed with elegant stylised gestures, either as a form of wrestling, or as fencing with a sword or a traditional *kris,* known as *pencak silat.*

Calendar of Events

Check precise dates before you leave, as the timing of Malaysia's many festivals tends to vary each year according to lunar calendars.

January/February. New Year's Day is a national public holiday.

Chinese New Year begins with a family dinner, and is accompanied by red banners and lion dances in Chinatown. Festivities end on the 15th day, Chap Goh Meh. KL, Penang, Kuching and KK are the best places for watching.

Hari Raya Puasa or Aidil-Fitri celebrations mark the end of Ramadan.

Thaipusam is the Hindu festival for Lord Murugan, celebrated with a procession of penitents seeking absolution at his shrine. The biggest is from KL to the Batu Caves *(see page 43)*.

March/April. Easter: Peninsular Eurasians and indigenous Christian converts in Sarawak and Sabah celebrate with Good Friday processions, most famously the Portuguese community of Melaka at St Peter's Church. Kelantan Kite Festival *(see page 88)*.

Chithirai Vishu (Hindu New Year), with worship and prayers.

May. Kadazans celebrate Tadau Kaamatan (Sabah Rice Harvest Festival).

Kota Belud Market Festival, with spectacular movements by Bajau cowboys.

May/June. Colours of Malaysia, a national celebration of cultural diversity.

June. Hari Gawai Dayak (Sarawak Rice Harvest Festival): Indigenous people of Sarawak get together for rice wine, feasting and festivities.

Festa de San Pedro (29 June): Boisterous Christian tribute to Peter, patron saint of fishermen, in Melaka.

July/August. Rainforest World Music Festival in Sarawak.

Festival of Hungry Ghosts: The Chinese honour their ancestors.

Hari Merdeka (National Day; 31 August) is a national public holiday.

October/November. Deepavali (Hindu Festival of Lights): Major Indian celebration, with candles lit, family feasts and prayers in the temple.

Prophet Mohammed's Birthday involves processions and recitals from the Qur'an.

Malaysian International Gourmet Festival throughout November.

December. KL International Buskers' Festival throughout December.

Christmas Day: Celebrated across Malaysia as a national public holiday.

EATING OUT

A meal in Malaysia can be as varied as the ethnic mix that makes up the country. Chinese, Indian, Indonesian and Thai recipes and ingredients all make their contribution. Malay cuisine itself is often a combination of all these and other ingredients as well.

In addition to hotel restaurants, you will find independent restaurants in the big cities, often perched on top of skyscrapers, offering panoramic views. Kuala Lumpur, Melaka, Ipoh and Penang's George Town all have high-quality Chinese and Indian restaurants and a few Malay ones. Smart-casual dress is all that is required in most. Meal times are also less rigid, especially as the popular hawkers' centres often serve meals all day long. Vegetarians need not worry: many Chinese and Indian shops offer various vegetarian dishes.

Food Stalls. The arena for a gastronomic adventure is the open-air food court. The stalls line both sides of a street or surround a court filled with tables, each offering different dishes of seafood, meat, chicken, vegetables, barbecue, soup, noodles or rice. Every town has its popular venues: in KL, there are Jalan Alor and Chinatown's Jalan Petaling; in Melaka, Melaka Raya; in Penang, Gurney Drive; in Ipoh, Jalan Yau Tet Shin; in Kota Bharu, Jalan Padang Garong; in Kuching, Lintang Batu.

Keep to the right

The left hand – and left-hand side – is considered to be impolite, and for Muslims eating with the left hand is viewed as unclean. Use the right hand for eating, greeting or handing anything to someone.

Find yourself a free table, note its number and begin your round of the hawkers, placing your orders. You can watch your meal being

Satay – possibly the world's most popular Malay dish

cooked right in front of you, or simply wait for the various dishes to be brought over to you.

WHAT TO EAT

Malay Cuisine

Like Indonesian cuisine with which it shares a common tradition, Malay cooking is rice-based, but the southern Chinese influence has also made noodles very popular.

The most common Malay dish is *satay* – pieces of chicken, beef or mutton (pork being forbidden, of course) skewered and cooked over charcoal. It is served in a spicy sauce of ground peanuts, peanut oil, chillis, garlic, onion, sugar and tamarind water, with slices of cucumber and glutinous rice wrapped in *ketupat* (palm leaves).

Mee rebus is a combination of noodles with beef, chicken or prawns and cubes of bean curd in a piquant brown gravy.

To say that *prawn sambal* is spicy would be an understatement. It is served with *nasi lemak* (rice steamed in coconut milk), chillis and condiments.

Tahu bakar, a soybean cake in a sweet, spicy peanut sauce with cucumber slices, is served on a nest of bean sprouts. Rice seasoned with lemon grass, chillis, ginger and soy accompanies *beef rendang*, pieces of beef marinated in coconut milk.

Otak otak is a grilled banana-leaf 'packet' of fish paste with coconut. Try *gula melaka sago* pudding with coconut milk and a syrup of palm sugar, or the colourful combination of *chendol* – coconut milk with red beans, green jelly and brown sugar.

Tropical Fruit

Malaysia may not be able to match France's 400 cheeses, but it does have 40 different kinds of bananas. The tiny ones are the sweetest, while the big green ones are used for cooking. Connoisseurs sing the praises of the three-panelled rather than the commoner four-panelled banana.

Besides the deliciously sweet watermelon and pineapple, there are some real exotica to be discovered. The largest of all is the huge pear-shaped jackfruit, hanging directly from the tree's trunk and main branches. Nicely tart in taste, the yellow flesh has a chewy consistency.

Without its hairy red skin, the white-fleshed rambutan is almost indistinguishable in taste from the lychee – delicious. The waxy yellow-skinned *carambola* (starfruit) does not look like a star until you cut it in slices. It is refreshingly tangy.

Once you get past the foul smell of durian, it really is very tasty. Addicts say 'Smell? What smell?' Spiky and big as a football, its flesh is rich and creamy, best of all in its wild state in the forest.

If you are a health fanatic, go for the vitamin-packed guava, green-skinned with white flesh, or papaya, green-skinned with orange pulp, or the sensual mango, growing, it seems, in a dozen different varieties in almost every Malaysian's back garden.

Malaysia's tropical fruit offerings include 40 kinds of banana

Chinese Cuisine

With the Chinese community so dominant in many of the towns, you will often find more Chinese than Malay restaurants and food stalls. Along with the staples of Chinese cooking, you will find a wide range of regional dishes in Malaysia.

Hokkien cooking specialises in noodles. Try *Hokkien-fried mee*, moist noodles with prawn, squid, pork and vegetables. *Or chien* is a seasoned omelette with tiny oysters and spring onions. In Klang and KL, Hokkien chefs make excellent *bah kut teh*, a soup of pork ribs, garlic and herbs. Eight-jewel chicken or duck, which is stewed and boned, is stuffed with diced pork, mushrooms, dried prawns, carrots and glutinous rice. Carrot cake is, in fact, more of an omelette made with a grated radish that the Chinese call 'white carrot'. Other Hokkien staples are *hay cho*, deep-fried balls of prawn, mashed pork and water chestnuts; and *popiah*, a rice-flour spring roll of shredded meat, turnip, bean sprouts, bean curd, prawn and garlic.

Teochew cooking is famous for its steamboat, a southern Chinese version of fondue – very big on KL's Jalan Petaling. Pieces of fish and seafood, meat, chicken and vegetables are dipped by each diner into hot stock in the bubbling 'steamboat' set in the centre of the table. At the end, the stock makes an excellent soup with which to finish the meal. Teochew cuisine is light and non-greasy, based principally on seafood. The fresh fish is sweet because it is first mixed with a very light mixture of sweet berry sauce, peanuts and sesame oil. *Or leon*, a Teochew dish, is boiled, sweetened yam.

A favourite hawker-stall noodle dish is *char kway teow*, with prawns, clams, bean sprouts and eggs fried in chilli and dark soy sauce. Ipoh claims its bean sprouts and noodles are

The street stalls on Jalan Alor serve some of KL's best food

the best on the peninsula, served with boiled chicken in a clear broth.

Hainan Island has contributed the great dish Hainanese chicken rice. The chicken is stuffed with ginger, boiled, and served in pieces

Local speciality

Walk through any Malaysian town mid-morning and the most crowded eateries will usually be those serving *roti canai,* a deliciously light, flaky pancake served with dhal.

with onion-flavoured rice and a special sauce of pounded chillis, lime juice and garlic. They also make a masterful *mutton soup* simmered with Chinese herbs, ginger and young bamboo shoots.

Nyonya Cuisine

This aromatic and spicy cuisine is a blend of Chinese and Malay traditions developed by descendants of the Chinese who intermarried in the Straits Settlements, Melaka and Penang. The result is a much spicier version of the many southern Chinese dishes mentioned above. Most famous in Penang is *Assam laksa,* a hot and sour fish-based noodle soup flavoured with tamarind, lemon grass and curry spices.

Bubor cha cha is a coconut milk creation with pieces of yam, sweet potato, sago and coloured gelatin. The Nyonya version of *otak otak,* a fish cake with coconut milk, lemon grass and shallots, wrapped in a palm leaf and grilled.

Indian Cuisine

The best Indian food stalls serve their curries, rice, fish, meat and vegetables piled high on a broad expanse of banana leaf. Indians may eat with their fingers, but you will be offered a fork and spoon if you wish.

Most of Malaysia's Indian community comes from the south of the subcontinent, where the searingly hot curries are sweetened by coconut milk. Chefs in North Indian

Sumptuous Malaysian food

restaurants tend to use a lot of yoghurt and a more subtle variety of spices. Since World War II, their numbers have been increased by Muslim immigrants from Pakistan and Bangladesh, who have added beef to the traditional mutton and chicken dishes. Many Hindu restaurants, particularly around the temples, are purely vegetarian, offering delicious variations on curried aubergine, tomatoes, potatoes, lentils and okra (lady's fingers), accompanied by traditional breads – *thosai, chapati, naan, roti canai* and, of course, *papadam*.

As universal now as Chinese food, the Indian and Indian-Muslim dishes you will come across in Malaysia include *biryani* (rice and meat, fish, or vegetables cooked together, with nuts, dried fruit and spices); *tandoori* (marinated pieces of chicken or fish baked in a clay oven); and *murtabak* (rice-dough pancakes, which are folded over chicken, beef or mutton, onion, eggs and vegetables). The latter can be a handy take-away snack but is better eaten at the table dipped in curry gravy.

Drinks

With all those exotic tropical fruits just dropping off the trees, the best drink here is a simple, fresh fruit juice – mango, lime, *carambola* (starfruit), watermelon, guava and pineapple being the most common. Malaysians like soy milk, often sold at markets in a balloon-like plastic bag with a straw. One of the cheapest local drinks is coconut water, from green king coconuts.

If you want a local brew, try the potent rice wine in Sarawak and Sabah. *Tuak* is the fermentation, *lankau* the processing with yeast. The local beer is very good, but imported beers like Heineken and Carlsberg are available.

To Help You Order…

Could we have a table? **Boleh dapatkan kami sebuah meja?**

I'd like a/an/some… **Saya hendak…**

bread	**roti**	meat	**daging**
butter	**mentega**	menu	**menu**
cheese	**keju**	milk	**susu**
coffee	**kopi**	mineral water	**air mineral**
eggs	**telur**	potatoes	**kentang**
fish	**ikan**	rice	**nasi**
fruit	**buah**	sugar	**gula**
ice	**ais**	tea	**teh**
ice cream	**ais krim**	vegetables	**sayur**

…and Read the Menu

ais krim	ice cream	**kastad karamel**	caramel custard
anggur	grapes		
ayam	chicken	**limau**	lemon
babi	pork	**nanas**	pineapple
bawang putih	garlic	**nasi goreng**	fried rice
bola daging	meatballs	**raspberi**	raspberries
cili hijau	green pepper	**sayur-sayuran**	vegetables
hati	liver	**sosej pedas**	spicy sausage
ikan	fish		
kacang	beans	**stek daging**	beefsteak
kambing	goat	**udang**	prawns

HANDY TRAVEL TIPS

An A–Z Summary of Practical Information

A

ACCOMMODATION (see also BUDGETING FOR YOUR TRIP)

In Malaysia, accommodation ranges from five-star luxury hotels run by international chains to the adequate *rumah tumpangan* (lodging house) – usually a shophouse converted into a hotel – and the really bare A-frame beach huts that offer comfort a notch above camping. The government regulates the industry by issuing licences to operate hotels and to sell alcohol. Most properties are rated by stars (1–5).

Hotels. International-standard hotels can be found in the state capitals and popular holiday spots. They offer marble floors, good service, clubs, live entertainment, swimming pools and restaurants serving Western, Chinese, Japanese or local food. Rack rates can be as high as RM1,000 and above but most are around RM200–500. Two- or three-star hotels offer the basics, which should be comfortable enough: many have air-conditioning, and most are safe and decent.

Budget rooms. Budget rooms styled after the bed-and-breakfast concept are available in KL, Melaka and Penang. These are relatively clean, though you may have to use a common shower and toilet. Lebuh Chulia in George Town is famed as a backpacker haunt.

Budget chalets. Another recent development is the mushrooming of budget chalets along Malaysia's scenic beaches. These can be found in resort islands like Langkawi, Pangkor and Tioman, and along east coast beaches like Cherating, Rantau Abang and Marang. These offer competitively priced rooms for those on a budget.

A bare room with a bed, clean sheets, shower and toilet could cost as little as RM40 a night. For extra money, some will include a mosquito net – a necessity for sound sleeping. In the absence of a mosquito net, the trick is to burn a mosquito coil. These are green coils that look like incense sticks, but whose rather acrid smoke deters mosquitoes. Otherwise, turn the ceiling fan to maximum. If that doesn't work, your last resort is to find air-conditioned accommodation, which will inevitably be more expensive.

Rest houses. These are bungalows formerly owned by English planters and civil servants, now turned into hotels with a colonial atmosphere. You will find them in the Cameron Highlands, Taiping, Fraser's Hill and some small towns. Most are now privately owned.

Youth hostels and YMCAs. Malaysia may not have an extensive network of youth hostels and YMCAs, but the few available are adequate and clean. Hostels run by the Malaysian Youth Hostels Association can be found in KL, Melaka and Port Dickson. An overnight stay in a youth hostel costs about RM30 in KL in dormitory accommodation and RM20 in Port Dickson and Melaka. Contact the Malaysian Youth Hostel Association, 1–7 Block B, Impian Kota Apartment, Jalan Manau, off Jalan Kampung Attap, 50460 **Kuala Lumpur**, tel: 03-2273 6870/71; www.myha.org.my; **Melaka** tel: 06-282 7915.

YMCAs can be found in Kuala Lumpur, George Town and Ipoh. The YMCA in KL offers the best value for money, with single air-conditioned rooms at RM66.

Kuala Lumpur: 95 Jalan Padang Belia; tel: 03-2274 1439.
George Town: 211 Jalan Macallister; tel: 04-228 8211.
Ipoh: 211 Jalan Raya Musa, A212; tel: 05-2540 809.

Please note that hotels are usually full during local festivals (see HOLIDAYS) and school holidays. Students go on holiday for a week in January/February, a week in March, three weeks in June, a week in August and five weeks in November/December.

AIRPORTS (see also GETTING THERE)

The major international airports are in Sepang (Kuala Lumpur International Airport or KLIA), Selangor, Subang (the 'old' KL airport), Bayan Lepas in Penang, Kuching in Sarawak, Labuan Island (an offshore financial centre off Sabah), and Kota Kinabalu in Sabah. You can also fly into Malaysia via Langkawi Island and Tioman Island.

KLIA (tel: 03-8777 8888; www.klia.com.my) offers the latest in airport systems and design, and is frequently rated as one of the most advanced in Southeast Asia. Capable of handling up to 25 million passengers a year, it is 75km (47 miles) from KL and connected to KL Sentral rail hub by the high-speed rail link ERL, a 28-minute ride for RM35. Transfers are also available by limousine or coach. Limousines cost about RM80, but sharing is possible. Coaches, which run regularly, are RM20. A transfer to your hotel comes at an additional charge. A budget taxi fare from the city to the airport is around RM75.

The journey from the city takes up to one hour even with the excellent expressway system and the vehicle travelling at the maximum 110km/h (69mph) speed limit.

Subang Airport is now largely used for private charters, Berjaya Air's flights to various resort islands and Firefly's to domestic airports.

Departure taxes (RM6 to domestic destinations, RM45 to everywhere else) are included in your ticket price.

ALCOHOL

There is no ban on alcohol in Malaysia. However, in certain states like Kelantan, Terengganu, Perlis and Kedah, there is stricter control on the sale of alcohol outside hotels because of the stronger Islamic influence in these predominantly Malay states. Muslims are not supposed to purchase alcohol from shops and restaurants.

In KL and larger cities, supermarkets and stores sell alcohol until 9pm. Pubs and bars may serve until 1am. Clubs stay open until 3am.

If you visit a Sarawak longhouse, the Ibans (natives of Sarawak) will welcome you at every doorway with a glass of *tuak,* a sweet wine made from glutinous rice. It certainly is a warm way of breaking the ice. Sabah has its own version of the potent wine, which is called *tapai.*

B

BUDGETING FOR YOUR TRIP

Travelling to Malaysia can be done on a wide range of budgets, whether you stay in a Chinese-run hotel in eastern Malaysia or a plush resort on Langkawi Island. A well-connected bus network supplements the extensive airlinks on the peninsula. Air transport and ferry lines in Sabah and Sarawak compensate where road transport is lacking.

Accommodation. A room at an expensive (4- or 5-star) hotel will cost from RM200–500 per night; for an average (2- or 3- star) hotel, expect to pay RM100–180 per night; for an economy room (no air-conditioning, perhaps with a shared bath) expect to pay RM30–40. Rooms in East Malaysia are sometimes more expensive.

Meals. Food in Malaysia is relatively inexpensive, and apart from high-end restaurants, you can eat well on a very modest budget. You will pay more at fancier places in KL and Penang. A meal for two at an expensive restaurant could cost as much as RM150–250; at a moderate restaurant expect to pay RM50–100; and if you eat at an inexpensive restaurant or food court, expect to pay RM30 or less.

Internal transportation. An express train trip rarely costs more than RM100; a flight from KL to Kuching in Sarawak or Kota Kinabalu in Sabah can cost RM300–600 depending on when you fly and how far in advance you purchase your ticket.

AirAsia offers budget flight services at unbeatable prices to domestic and international destinations. Details at www.airasia.com.

Sightseeing. Admission to museums is often free or at least very inexpensive (RM1–2). More costly are national parks, particularly if you need to hire guides. Entry permits may be as little as RM6 for Taman Negara (including a camera permit); a guided walk may cost RM40; a guide will cost around RM150 per day. At Mount Kinabalu, a climbing permit is RM50, with additional charges for insurance and guides. Transport will add to these charges, particularly if hiring a boat.

C

CAMPING

There is no organised network for campers but camping is a good and cheap option in Malaysia. Campsites are available within the major nature parks like Lake Chini, Taman Negara (National Park) in Pahang, and the Bukit Cahaya Seri Alam Park in Shah Alam, Selangor, should you venture this far from the city centre. A two-person tent can be hired for RM6 per night and a four-person tent for around RM12. You have to pay a small fee to register as a camper at Taman Negara. For more information, check with local tourism authorities or park authorities in the state capitals you may be visiting. Some popular camping sites are found at:

Taman Negara, Pahang: Wildlife and National Parks Department, Km 10, Jalan Cheras, 56100 Kuala Lumpur; tel: 03-9075 2872; email: pakp@wildlife.gov.my; www.wildlife.gov.my.

Endau Rompin National Park: National Parks (Johor) Corporation, JKR 475, Bukit Timbalan, 82503 Johor Bahru, Johor; tel: 07-223 7471; email: jnpc@johorpark.com; www.johorpark.com.

CAR HIRE (see also DRIVING)

Several car hire companies, including some international names, are based in major cities and listed in the *Yellow Pages*. You will also find car hire counters at most airports including: KLIA, Penang, Ipoh, Johor Bahru, Kuantan, Kuching, Kota Kinabalu, Bintulu, Miri and Langkawi.

Rates range from RM150–700 daily, depending on the make and engine capacity of the car. A Proton Wira 1.3 can be hired at RM150–60 per day with unlimited mileage. A Mercedes Benz 200 will cost about RM700 per day with unlimited mileage. Major credit cards are accepted. The car will usually be delivered with a full tank of petrol and must be filled up before you hand it back. You need either an international driving licence or a valid licence from your own country. In most cases, drivers must be over 25 years of age.

CLIMATE

Malaysia is a tropical country, and the heat and humidity can take its toll on the unsuspecting, especially if you have just departed from a country in the midst of winter. In general, the Malaysian climate is hot, humid and wet. Daily lowland temperatures range from 21–32°C (70–90°F). Rainfall averages 250cm (98in) annually. Nights can be cool, but the day is usually hot.

Monsoon rains bring heavy showers. The northeast monsoon lasts from November until February; most affected are the east coast states of Kelantan, Terengganu and Pahang, and parts of Sabah. Some parts of the country may become isolated during the monsoon, but this is usually only temporary. The southwest monsoon lasts from July until September. The rain is not as heavy because of the shielding effect of the Indonesian island of Sumatra.

It is not advisable to swim in the sea or travel in small boats off the east coast during the northeast monsoon. Other than that, the seas in Malaysia are generally safe for swimming, sailing and water sports.

CLOTHING

Since the climate is hot, humid and wet, you should wear thin, light-coloured, loose clothing, preferably made of cotton. At the hill resorts, a sweater will suffice to keep you warm.

Malaysians dress in a relaxed manner, even at fancy restaurants. At a formal occasion, a suit and tie or a long-sleeved batik shirt will do (this garment will get you into any respectable establishment in Malaysia, including the casino in Genting Highlands). However, sandals and slippers are too casual for restaurants and clubs. At the beach, anything goes except for topless or nude sunbathing. For walking around, wear a pair of rubber-soled shoes or good walking boots, and wear cotton or wool socks (since you are bound to sweat). Remember to take off your shoes before entering a home or place of worship. Malaysians usually take off their shoes before entering their homes and sometimes offices. Refrain from wearing shorts or short skirts when visiting mosques and rural areas, especially in the east coast states. Clothing can be purchased in Malaysia for very reasonable prices, but larger sizes can be hard to find.

Dressing for the rainforest. It is important to pack light when preparing to visit a rainforest, as it is more humid and you can easily get tired. Be prepared to get wet, so a light raincoat is a must. Line your backpack with a plastic bag and check that everything is waterproof, as river crossings are almost inevitable. Long-sleeved cotton shirts and cotton trousers are comfortable and will help to protect you from insects and thorny undergrowth.

If you are visiting mountain peaks, such as Mount Mulu or Mount Kinabalu, be aware that temperatures can drop to 0°C (32°F), so be sure to bring warmer clothing and even gloves. It is worth packing a water bottle, purifying tablets (or a receptacle to boil all your water), insect repellent, sunscreen, a cap, small towel or sarong and energy supplements, such as chocolate. Anti-leech socks are useful too.

CRIME AND SAFETY (see also Emergencies and Police)

Malaysia is generally safe, but as in any other country, some basic rules apply. Petty theft occurs in tourist areas, and some consular warnings point to a high rate of credit card fraud and snatch thieves.
• Don't accept drinks from strangers.
• Don't carry too much money in your wallet.
• Don't flaunt expensive jewellery.
• Don't leave your bags or cameras lying around unattended.
• When visiting crowded places, beware of pickpockets.
• Dress in a sensible manner.

CUSTOMS AND ENTRY REQUIREMENTS

To enter Malaysia, you need a valid passport or visa. A disembarkation card has to be filled out and handed to Immigration officials on arrival. Even though Sabah and Sarawak are in the federation of Malaysia, you need a passport to visit these East Malaysian States.
Visa requirements. British, Irish and most Commonwealth citizens do not need a visa. Holders of US passports, for example, can enter Malaysia for three months without a visa.

Export of antiques and historical objects is not allowed unless an export licence is obtained from the Director General of Museums Malaysia or if the antique was originally imported and declared to Customs upon arrival.

Foreign tourists must declare to Customs or the Plant Quarantine inspector any flowers, plants, fruit, seeds, soil samples, cultures of fungi, bacteria or viruses, and insects or any other vertebrate or invertebrate animals in their possession, as well as if they have visited any country in tropical America or the Caribbean during the previous 30 days. In effect, the quarantine officers are quite relaxed about the importation of these materials.

Visitors older than 18 years entering Malaysia for more than 72 hours may purchase the following items tax-free:

• Not more than 225g of tobacco or 200 cigarettes or 50 cigars.
• Not more than one litre of wine, spirits/malt liqueur.
• Not more than RM200-worth of souvenirs and gifts.

Visitors to Langkawi and other duty-free ports can purchase as they like if travelling directly overseas from the duty-free port. However, if travelling domestically back into other Malaysian states, duty-free limitations apply.

Warning: The trafficking of illegal drugs is a serious offence in Malaysia, and the penalty for such an offence is death.

D

DRIVING (see also TRANSPORT)

In Malaysia, driving is on the left – a legacy of British colonialism. Road signs are in Malaysian.

The highway code is of the universal type, with distances and speed limits are in kilometres. The speed limit varies with the road conditions: it ranges from 90–110 km/h (56–68 mph) on highways and from 30–80 km/h (18–50 mph) in urban areas and town limits. Speed cameras and radar guns are used to nab speeders. Check the speed limit signs regularly. It is illegal to use mobile phones while driving.

Accelerated growth combined with a lack of planning has led to confusing road systems in Kuala Lumpur and other major towns. After a while you'll find some sense in the confusion. Most roads are named, except for satellite towns like Petaling Jaya where numbers are used.

Roads are generally of good quality, and the North–South Expressway, which links Singapore to Thailand, is of international standard, though you have to pay a toll to use it.

E

ELECTRICITY

The voltage is 220 volts throughout Malaysia. Electricity is widely available except in remote areas and some islands where generators are used.

Note: You will find square or round three-pin plugs in different establishments, while some old hotels use two-pin plugs. Fused adapters are easily available in department and hardware stores; they cost around RM5 each. A universal adapter is handy.

EMBASSIES AND CONSULATES

Unless otherwise noted, all are in Kuala Lumpur.

Australia	6 Jalan Yap Kwan Seng; tel: 03-2146 5555.
Canada	17th Floor, Menara Tan & Tan, 207 Jalan Tun Razak; tel: 03-2718 3333.
New Zealand	21st Floor, Menara IMC, No. 8, Jalan Sultan Ismail; tel: 03-2078 2533.
UK	185 Jalan Ampang; tel: 03-2170 2200.
US	376 Jalan Tun Razak; tel: 03-2168 5000.

Where is the … consulate?   **Dimanakah konsulat …?**

EMERGENCIES

Dial 999 if you need to contact the police or ambulance services, or 994 for the fire and rescue services. Major hotels offer medical services for minor ailments.

G

GAY AND LESBIAN TRAVELLERS

Homosexuality is illegal under Malaysian law. Nevertheless, gay life is tolerated throughout the country, although discretion is strongly advised, especially in popular meeting places. For further information on this subject, visit www.utopia-asia.com/tipsmala.htm.

GETTING THERE (see also AIRPORTS)

Flying is the most common means of getting to Malaysia, and KLIA is the major gateway; you will sometimes find cheaper fares to Singapore or Bangkok, and from either of these gateways you can get to Malaysia by train or plane. The national airline, Malaysia Airlines, flies from numerous destinations around the world. Many airlines like KLM, Singapore Airlines and Cathay Pacific all fly to KLIA. Budget airline AirAsia also connects to the region. Fares are best booked online. Check with the closest Tourism Malaysia Office or travel agent for more specific information. Many people travel to Malaysia quite economically on packages or tours.

GUIDES AND INTERPRETERS

Professional guides normally work for tour companies that organise inbound tours; few work independently. You may decide to discover Malaysia on your own, but tours or treks into the more remote parts of the country do benefit from the assistance of a guide. Most people make arrangements with tour companies in advance of their trip. Contact a Tourism Malaysia office in your home country and they will advise on the most reputable companies. If you don't make arrangements in advance of your trip, you will find most of the tour companies in such major destinations as KL, Penang, Kuching, Kota Kinabalu, Langkawi and Sandakan.

Since English is widely spoken, tourists from English-speaking countries should encounter few language barriers.

H

HEALTH AND MEDICAL CARE

Most major hotels and resorts provide some medical service for minor ailments. Every town has a government hospital and major towns and cities have private clinics and hospitals. Doctors, nurses and other medical staff mostly speak English, and chances are high that they will have obtained their qualifications from Western universities.

If you have a sensitive stomach, do be cautious when ordering food and drink from hawkers' stalls. Though the tap water is chlorinated, drink boiled or bottled water. Lay off curries and spicy foods unless you're used to such exotic fare.

Pharmacies, many of which are located in department stores, close at 9pm.

Health regulations. A valid vaccination certificate against yellow fever is required from any traveller above one year of age who has visited a yellow fever-infected country up to six days prior to arrival in Malaysia.

If you plan to trek in the forest, take anti-malaria pills. It is also advisable to be vaccinated against Hepatitis B or at least to have a gamma-globulin injection prior to your trip.

HOLIDAYS

Malaysia has numerous public holidays as a consequence of its multicultural population and their respective religious practices. These holidays vary from year to year and are as follows:

1 January	New Year's Day
January/February	Chinese New Year (two days)
	Hindu festival of Thaipusam
March/April	Good Friday (in Sabah and Sarawak)
1 May	Labour Day
6 May	Wesak Day, a time of prayer for Buddhists
30–31 May	Kaamatan Harvest Festival in Sabah
1–2 June	Gawai Harvest Festival in Sarawak
6 June	King's Birthday
June/July	Hari Raya Haji (dates subject to change)
	First day of Muharram
31 August	National Day
August/September	Prophet Mohammed's Birthday
November	Hindu festival of Deepavali (except Sabah and Sarawak); Muslim festival of Hari Raya Aidil Fitri (two days, dates subject to change)
25 December	Christmas Day

If a public holiday falls at the end or beginning of a week, many Malaysians take advantage of the long weekend to have an extended holiday. At such times, it can be difficult to book hotels, taxis or train, plane or bus tickets, so make sure you book well in advance.

Furthermore, Malaysians working in urban areas traditionally return to their villages (a practice called *balik kampung*) to celebrate festivals like Chinese New Year, Hari Raya Aidil Fitri and Deepavali. Try not to travel during these *balik kampung* periods as traffic becomes very congested.

L

LANGUAGE

Bahasa Malaysia, or Malay, is the national language. Tamil is the main Indian dialect spoken in Malaysia, and Mandarin and many Chinese dialects are also spoken. But English is widely known and used as well; there shouldn't be any communication problems unless you are in a remote area. Most signs are written in romanised Malay.

Do you speak English/German/French?	Boleh-kah awak bercakap bahasa Inggeris/Jerman/Perancis?
I don't understand.	Saya tidak faham.
You're welcome.	Sama-sama.
Excuse me (I'm sorry).	Maafkan saya.
Help me, please.	Tolong bantu saya.
How are you?	Apa khabar?
Very well, thank you	Sangat baik, terima kasih.
good morning	selamat pagi
good evening	selamat petang
good night	selamat malam
goodbye	selamat tinggal
no entrance	tidak boleh masuk
no photos	tidak boleh ambil gambar
no smoking	tidak boleh hisap rokok
please	tolong
thank you	terima kasih
yes (correct)	betul
no (incorrect)	salah
road/street	jalan/lebuh
hill	bukit
church	gereja
temple	kuil
mosque	masjid
palace	istana
park	taman
entrance	masuk
exit	keluar
closed	tutup

M

MAPS

Tourism Malaysia publishes maps of various places of interest in Malaysia. You can find these at hotels, tourist information centres, major airports and train stations. More detailed maps can be purchased at petrol stations and leading bookshops.

MEDIA

Local English-language newspapers are *New Straits Times, The Malay Mail, The Star* and *The Sun*, available at all newsstands, with *The Sun* being free. In Sabah and Sarawak you will also find local English-language editions of *The New Sabah Times* and *Sarawak Tribune*. Newsagents in leading hotels and major bookshops sell foreign newspapers at relatively high prices, often arriving very late. Special-interest magazines in English are available.

Radio broadcasts exist in Malay, Mandarin, English and Tamil. There are six TV stations: three are government-owned and the rest are privately run. Major hotels have in-house video programmes. All TV stations feature popular Western programmes in English with Malay subtitles. Satellite or cable TV is widely available via Astro.

MEETING PEOPLE

Malaysians are very hospitable and friendly. Say hello and they will immediately return your greeting and possibly strike up a conversation. In certain popular areas like Tioman Island, Cherating Bay in Pahang, Marang in Terengganu and Langkawi Island, many villagers have converted their homes into budget chalets, enabling visitors to experience to some degree the Malaysian way of life. Tourism Malaysia has initiated a homestay programme and many villagers have joined. Check www.tourismmalaysia.com for specific locations.

Some tour companies offer visits to Malaysian homes during festivals like the Chinese New Year and Hari Raya Aidil Fitri (a Muslim festival marking the end of Ramadan). Malaysians celebrate festivals by having open houses for neighbours, friends and relatives.

Some taboos. Malays don't like pointing or being pointed at with forefingers; point with your thumb instead. They also feel it is not courteous to hand over or receive things with the left hand; make it a point to use your right hand whenever possible.

MONEY

The official name for the monetary unit is Ringgit Malaysia (RM). One hundred sen make one Ringgit. *Coins:* 5, 10, 20 and 50 sen coins. *Banknotes:* RM1, RM5, RM10, RM20, RM50 and RM100.

Keep 10-sen coins for local phone calls. To make lots of calls, buy a phone card. Vending machines take 10-, 20- and 50-sen coins; some accept RM1 notes. Parking meters take 10-, 20- and 50-sen coins.

Banks and currency exchange. Travellers' cheques are accepted at all banks. Major credit cards can be used at most hotels, department stores and some shops. Currency can be exchanged at banks or licensed money-changers, which operate beyond banking hours (most licensed money-changers close by 8pm). Exchange rates vary, so shop around.

1	satu	20	dua puluh
2	dua	21	dua puluh satu
3	tiga	30	tiga puluh
4	empat	40	empat puluh
5	lima	50	lima puluh
6	enam	60	enam puluh
7	tujuh	70	tujuh puluh
8	lapan	80	lapan puluh
9	sembilan	90	sembilan puluh
10	sepuluh	100	seratus
11	sebelas	200	dua ratus
12	dua belas	1,000	seribu

Currency restrictions. The Malaysian Government imposed currency controls in September 1999. Under the controls the Malaysian Ringgit was tied to a rate of around RM3.3 to the US dollar. After several years which saw the currency and economy stabilise, the restrictions were eased in 2005, and the Ringgit is no longer pegged to the US dollar.

Residents and non-residents have to declare the exact amount of Ringgit they are taking into or out of the country if it exceeds RM10,000. Residents are required to declare in detail the exact amount in foreign currency they are carrying if the amount exceeds the equivalent of RM10,000, but they do not have to declare the amount of foreign currency they are holding when entering Malaysia.

Non-residents have to declare in detail foreign currencies brought into or out of Malaysia only if the amount exceeds US$2,500.

OPENING HOURS

Malaysia has a dual system regarding the opening hours of government offices. In the States of Kelantan, Terengganu and Kedah, the weekend is on Friday and Saturday. Government offices open Sun–Thur 8am–4.30pm, Thur until 12.45pm. Banks open Sun–Wed and alternate Saturdays 9.30am–4pm, Thur 9.30–11.30am.

In the states of Selangor, Perak, Negeri Sembilan, Pahang, Melaka, Johor, Perlis, Penang, Sabah and Sarawak, government offices open Mon–Fri 8am–4.30pm. Banks open Mon–Fri 9.30am–4pm and alternate Saturdays 9.30–11.30am. The lunch break is longer on Friday because of prayer time for Muslims.

Generally, the private sector in Malaysia follows normal hours. Company offices open Mon–Fri 9am–5pm, Sat 9am–1pm. Post offices open Mon–Sat 8am–5pm (KL's GPO until 6pm), except in Kelantan, Kedah and Terengganu, where they close on Friday and open on Sunday.

Shops open daily until 7 or 8pm while major department stores open until 9.30 or 10pm. Most museums close at 6pm.

P

PHOTOGRAPHY

From the beauty of nature deep in the forest to white sands washed by clear seas, Malaysia is a photographer's paradise.

The processing of digital images and film is cheap and professional. Cities and large towns have digital imaging shops. Malaysia is also a good place to buy cameras, as the range is extensive and they are competitively priced.

The sunlight in Malaysia can be harsh, so the best periods to take pictures are in the mornings and evenings. Furthermore, be careful with your exposure readings; overexposure is a frequent occurrence.

You can photograph anything except some Malay women and children on the east coast who are quite shy. Avoid taking photographs of Muslims praying in mosques. Photography in museums, some shopping malls, art galleries, airports and military installations may be restricted, so check first.

POLICE (see also CRIME AND SAFETY)

Police stations can be found in almost every city and town in Malaysia. Policemen and women wear dark-blue uniforms.

POST OFFICES

The General Post Office in KL is open Mon–Sat 8am–6pm. On Sundays, the GPOs in KL, Penang, Johor Bahru, Ipoh, Kuantan, Melaka, Kuching and Kota Kinabalu open 10am–1pm. Those in other towns are open Mon–Sat 8am–5pm, except in Kelantan, Kedah and Terengganu where they close on Friday and open on Sunday. Stamps are sold at post offices and hotels, but letters can be dropped into red post boxes found everywhere. Major hotels will post your letters for you.

Malaysia has an express mail system (available at major post offices) called *Pos Laju,* which offers domestic delivery within 24 hours; other express services operate to overseas destinations.

R

RELIGION

Malaysia's traditional tolerance is accompanied by a mutual respect, which foreign visitors should also observe, most importantly with regard to taboos and dress restrictions. You should, therefore, remove your shoes on entering a mosque, or Buddhist or Hindu temple, as shoes are considered to bear the impurities of the outside world. This restriction may also apply to private homes – if you are not sure, do not be afraid to ask your host. In any case, you should not enter places of worship dressed for the beach. Muslims lend covering robes for women who are bare-shouldered or wearing shorts or skirts above the knees. Food taboos are less strictly imposed, but you should avoid ordering a pork dish when dining with Muslims or beef with Hindus. There is no restriction on photography at places of worship, but discretion is important as some may not like being photographed.

T

TELEPHONES

Telephone cards are in use in Malaysia, and some public phones can be used only with such cards. Coin-operated telephones still exist, but these are for local calls only. Out-of-state calls can be made by dialling area codes or with operator assistance. International calls can be made at major hotels, IDD call centres and Telekom Malaysia offices in major towns. International direct dialling, home country direct service and fax services are available at Telekom outlets in KLIA. Home country direct service is also available at the KL Sentral Station. Most Malaysians use mobile phones.

Here are some useful dialling codes:

Country code:	60	Operator:	101
International call prefix:	00	Directory enquiries:	103

TIME ZONES

Malaysian time is eight hours ahead of GMT, so when it is 1pm in Kuala Lumpur, it is 5am in London, midnight in Washington, DC and Ottawa, and 3pm in Canberra.

TIPPING

Tipping is not encouraged, but some trishaw riders, taxi drivers and tourist guides may want a reward. At major restaurants and hotels, a 10 percent service charge (plus 5 percent government tax) is added.

TOILETS

Public toilets are not always clean and often do not provide tissue paper; many are also in a state of disrepair. Be prepared to use squat toilets if you are not staying in Western-style establishments. Shopping complexes in KL and major towns normally charge for use of toilets (RM20–30 sen); these are much cleaner, and tissue paper is sold at the counter. Toilets at rest areas along the North–South Expressway provide paper, are free and generally clean.

toilets	**bilik air**
gentlemen/ladies	**lelaki/perempuan**

TOURIST INFORMATION *(Maklumat Pelancong)*

Offices of Tourism Malaysia exist in the countries listed below:
Australia
Level 2, 171 Clarence Street, Sydney, NSW 2000; tel: 02-9299 4441/2/3.
Ground Floor, 56 William Street, Perth, WA 6000; tel: 08-9481 0400.

Canada
Malaysian Tourist Information Centre, 1590–1111 West Georgia Street, Vancouver BC V6E 4M3; tel: 604-689 8899; toll-free 1-888 689 6872.

United Kingdom
57 Trafalgar Square, London WC2N 5DU; tel: 020-7930 7932.

US
• 818 West Seventh Street, Suite 970, Los Angeles, CA 90017; tel: 213-689 9702; toll-free 1-800 336 6842.

• 120 East 56th Street, Suite 810, New York, NY 10022; tel: 212-745 1114/5; toll-free 1-800 558 6787.

• **Embassy of Malaysia:** 3516 International Court, NW, Washington DC 20008; tel: 202-572 9700.

In Malaysia, there are several Tourist Information Offices:

Kuala Lumpur
Level 2, Menara Dato Onn, Putra World Trade Centre, Jalan Tun Ismail 50480, Kuala Lumpur; tel: 03-2693 5188.

Sabah
Pejabat LPPM Cawangan Sabah, Ground Floor, Bangunan EON CMG Life, No. 1, Jalan Sagunting, 88000 Kota Kinabalu; tel: 088-248 698/211 732.

Sarawak
Pejabat LPPM Cawangan Sawawak, 2nd floor, Bangunan, Rugayah, Jalan Sang Thian Cheok, 93100 Kuching; tel: 082-246 575/775.

In KL, get information and make bus, air, tour and hotel bookings at the Malaysia Tourism Centre on **Jalan Ampang**; tel: 03-2164 3929.

TRANSPORT (see also Driving)

By car. Roads are generally good except in parts of Sabah and Sarawak. The new North–South Expressway that links Singapore to south Thailand has made travelling by road much easier and faster.

By train. The KTM (*Keretapi Tanah Melayu*; www.ktmb.com.my), based in KL Sentral, offers an efficient rail service with reasonable fares across the country and to Thailand and Singapore. A railway line runs the whole length of Peninsular Malaysia to the Thai and Singapore borders. Another line links Gemas to Tumpat in the northeastern state of Kelantan. In Sabah, there is a railway line that links Kota Kinabalu to Tenom. The Kuala Lumpur to Singapore service is often fully booked. There is also an electric train service connecting Rawang, Seremban and Klang to the transport hub of KL Sentral.

By bus. Buses also ply the main towns. There are several companies, and tickets can be purchased at the generally very busy bus stations. It is best to book a day ahead. In remote places, the service is not regular and it is better to use taxis.

Mini-bus services are also available between popular destinations, and the fares are quite reasonable (RM10–20). Inter-city travel is cheap and convenient as major towns in Malaysia are connected by buses and air-conditioned express coaches to Singapore and Thailand. Aeroline (www.aeroline.com.my) operates business-class buses to Singapore for RM160 return.

By plane. Malaysia Airlines, Berjaya Air, AirAsia and Firefly operate an extensive network of domestic flights to all major towns in Malaysia, as well as to more remote places in Sabah and Sarawak.

By boat. Though a bridge now connects Penang island to the mainland, the quaint ferry service is still in operation and offers a much more colourful and enjoyable way to reach the island. There are also regular ferry services from Lumut to the resort island of Pangkor, from Kuala Perlis and Kuala Kedah to the holiday destination of Langkawi, from Mersing to the scenic Tioman Island and nearby isles, from Kuala Besut to the Perhentian and Redang Islands, from Kota Kinabalu to Labuan, and from Marang to Kapas Island.

Local transport. Cities and towns are serviced by buses. A Light Rail Transport system and monorail operates in KL and several adjoining suburbs. Taxis, mostly air-conditioned, are readily available and fares are metered, though in some places, like Penang, cabbies do not use the meter. In such places, negotiate the fare before boarding. In cities, taxis can be found at taxi stands or flagged down anywhere.

In the east coast towns of Kuala Terengganu and Kota Bharu, trishaws are a popular mode of transport. Sometimes gaudily decorated, they make for good photos. West coast towns like George Town in Penang and Melaka also have trishaws. Rides within town limits range from RM3–20, depending on the distance.

WATER

Tap water is treated with fluoride and is safe for drinking. As a precaution, drink boiled water, especially in rural areas. Bottled mineral water can be purchased in major towns.

WEBSITES

News:
www.thestar.com.my *The Star* newspaper
Tourism:
www.allmalaysia.info
www.tourismmalaysia.gov.my
www.sarawaktourism.com
www.sabahtourism.com
Travel:
www.klia.com.my Kuala Lumpur International Airport
www.ktmb.com.my Keretapi Tanah Melayu (Malaysian Rail)

WEIGHTS AND MEASURES

Malaysia uses the metric system.

Recommended Hotels

Although room rates have been slowly creeping up, Malaysian hotels can compete with the world's best and guests delight in the value offered. While resort islands manage to command consistently high rates, competition in KL keeps prices low on a global scale.

The monsoon affects various parts of the country at different times of year, but inconsistent arrivals in recent years have made this unpredictable. Normally the arrival of the rains on the east coast, for example, drives rates down from October to April. Apart from Malaysian public and school holidays, the high season in Malaysia tends to be during the European winter (Dec to Feb). Langkawi and Penang hotels are normally full during this period and early bookings are essential. Don't come to KL during the Formula 1 in March expecting discounted rates.

Most hotels are rated by Tourism Malaysia from one to five stars. The only rooms visitors would want to stay in are those that are air-conditioned. All but small establishments charge 10 percent service charge and 5 percent government tax (the latter is not applicable in Langkawi). Rack rates displayed in hotels should always be used as a guide and asking for promotional rates is recommended. Many guests shop around on the internet or use travel agents who can guarantee lower rates. Most hotels accept several credit cards.

$$$$	over US$120
$$$	US$80–120
$$	US$45–80
$	less than US$45

KUALA LUMPUR

Bintang Warisan $ *68 Jalan Bukit Bintang, 55100 Kuala Lumpur, tel: 03-2148 8111, fax: 03-2148 2333, www.bintangwarisan.com.* This centrally-located 10-storey budget hotel is in the middle of all the lively Bukit Bintang action, just 100m (330ft) from the monorail station. The busy lobby is forgotten once guests reach their comfortable and value-for-money rooms. Arguably the best budget hotel in the city centre. 97 rooms.

Hotel Capitol $$ *Jalan Bulan, off Jalan Bukit Bintang, 55100 Kuala Lumpur, tel: 03-2143 7000, fax: 03-2143 0000, www.fhihotels.com.* Good mid-range hotel in a central location close to shopping malls and entertainment outlets. The design is contemporary with several smart loft-styled suites on the upper two floors. 235 rooms.

Carcosa Seri Negara $$$$ *Taman Tasek Perdana, 50480 Kuala Lumpur, tel: 03-2295 0888, fax: 03-2282 7888, www.ghmhotels. com.* It's the Queen of England's preferred address – she stayed here when last in Malaysia. The boutique property has suites that retain their heritage value while incorporating contemporary facilities such as wireless internet throughout the two mansions. The landscaped gardens make for a special stay. Dine on contemporary French fare in The Dining Room, enjoy traditional English afternoon teas or try the local cuisine at the Gulai House. 13 suites.

Crown Princess $$ *City-Square Centre, Jalan Tun Razak, 50400 Kuala Lumpur, tel: 03-2162 5522, fax: 03-2162 4492, www.fhi hotels.com.* A well-established five-star hotel adjoining a shopping centre and within a 1km (0.6 mile) walk of KLCC. The rooms have been refurbished to offer a comfortable stay. Dine in excellent award-winning restaurants like the Taj (Indian), Spring Garden (Chinese) and Prime Grill (steaks and seafood). 576 rooms.

Hotel Equatorial $$$ *Jalan Sultan Ismail, 50250 Kuala Lumpur, tel: 03-2161 7777, fax: 03-2161 9020, www.equatorial.com/kul.* A smart, compact hotel within walking distance of most city attractions. Being Malaysian-owned, there's a warm welcome and professionalism shown by the staff. It has a strong reputation for food and wine with offerings like Flo (lounge and wine bar), Kampachi (Japanese), Chalet (classic European) and Golden Phoenix (Chinese). 300 rooms.

Nikko Kuala Lumpur $$$ *165 Jalan Ampang, 50450 Kuala Lumpur, tel: 03-2161 1111, fax: 03-2161 1122, www.hotelnikko.com.my.* Well located along embassy row and just 10 minutes' walk to KLCC and five to Ampang Park Putra Station. Elegant five-star rooms and some excellent restaurants – Benkay (Japanese), Toh Lee (Chinese) and Bentley's Bar (English pub) – complete this 30-storey hotel. 473 rooms.

Royale Bintang Damansara $$$ *6 Jalan PJU 7/3, Mutiara Daman-sara, 47800 Petaling Jaya, Selangor, tel: 03-7843 1111, fax: 03-7843 1122, www.royale-bintang-hotel.com.my.* This recently opened hotel is located in the up-market suburban retail heartland of KL adjacent to The Curve – ideal for those who like to be close to shops, restaurants, bars and cinemas. The compact rooms are smartly decorated and include broadband internet in each room. The adjoining mall offers a United Nations of culinary experiences. 145 rooms.

Traders Hotel Kuala Lumpur $$$ *Kuala Lumpur City Centre, 50088 Kuala Lumpur, tel: 03-2332 9888, fax: 03-2332 2666, www. tradershotels.com.* Possibly the best value four-star hotel in KL with a great KLCC location and within walking distance of all the Bukit Bintang retail action. Choose park view rooms and visit the SkyBar on the 33rd floor for KL's best evening views of the Twin Towers. Dine in Gobo Upstairs for superb steaks and fine wines. 571 rooms.

The Westin Kuala Lumpur $$$$ *199 Jalan Bukit Bintang, 55100 Kuala Lumpur, tel: 03-2731 8333, fax: 03-2773 8406, www.westin.com/kualalumpur.* Classy, contemporary-styled hotel in the epicentre of KL's retail and entertainment district. The Westin offers one of the best five-star experiences in KL and some fine restaurants like Prego (Italian), EEST (modern pan-Asian) and a trendy club called Qba. The hotel is within metres of shopping malls like the Pavilion, Starhill and Lot 10. 452 rooms.

PENANG

Cheong Fatt Tze Mansion $$$ *14 Leith Street, 10200 Penang, tel: 04-262 0006, fax: 04-262 5289, www.cheongfatttzemansion.com.* A former private mansion now restored as a boutique heritage property. Known as the 'Blue Mansion', its handful of rooms surround a central courtyard and all have been faithfully renovated and decorated with period furniture. 16 rooms.

Eastern & Oriental $$$$ *10 Lebuh Farquhar, 10200 Penang, tel: 04-222 2000, fax: 04-261 6333, www.e-o-hotel.com.* Possibly Malaysia's most celebrated heritage property, dating from 1885 when it was considered 'the finest hotel east of the Suez'. Renovations have maintained the historic fabric while incorporating contemporary facilities. All suites are spacious retreats with period furniture. Enjoy drinks in Farquhar's Bar and dine on Western cuisine in 1885 Restaurant. 101 suites.

Shangri-La Rasa Sayang Resort & Spa $$$$ *Batu Feringgi Beach, 1100 Penang, tel: 04-888 8888, fax: 04-881 1800, www.shangri-la.com/rasasayang.* The 'Shang' is an institution amongst the beachfront resorts of Batu Feringgi. Recent renovations have projected the well-established resort well into the 21st century. Relax in the Tibetan-inspired CHI, The Spa at Shangri-La or swim in the resort's two stunning pools. 304 rooms.

LANGKAWI

Bon Ton Resort Langkawi $$$ *Pantai Cenang, 07000 Langkawi, Kedah, tel: 04-955 3643, fax: 04-955 4791, www.bontonresort. com.my.* Chic and contemporary island design meets Malay heritage in this intimate resort comprising antique wooden Malay homes. During the day, couples lounge around the pool. At sunset, cocktails are served in the gardens and then dinner of 'west meets spice' cuisine continues through the evening. This is a gem that all visitors to Malaysia need to discover. Eight chalets.

Four Seasons $$$$ *Jalan Tanjung Rhu, 07000 Langkawi, Kedah, tel: 04-950 8888, fax: 04-950 8899, www.fourseasons.com.* Architecturally stunning, this luxurious property sets the standard in Langkawi. With just 91 villas and pavilions, guests get the best service. Relax in the Moorish-inspired spa, partake of sunset drinks in the Rhu Bar and enjoy fresh seafood in Ikan Ikan. Golf carts ferry guests around the various parts of this expansive and lushly landscaped resort.

Frangipani Langkawi Resort & Spa $$$$ *Jalan Teluk Baru, Pantai Tengah, 07100 Langkawi, Kedah, tel: 04-952 0000, fax: 04-952 0001, www.frangipanilangkawi.com.* This resort has a strong environmental bias with green management practices in place and is ideal for those who want to commune with nature. With 400m (1,300ft) of absolute beachfront, the swimming and sunbathing is just as inviting. Most rooms are located in separate or twin chalets amongst tropical gardens within seconds of the beach. Sunsets from the beach bar are spectacular. Great for families but also with superb honeymoon facilities. 118 rooms.

Meritus Pelangi Beach Resort & Spa $$$ *Pantai Cenang, 07000 Langkawi, Kedah, tel: 04-952 8888, fax: 04-955 8899, www. pelangibeachresort.com.* This village-styled retreat is well maintained and always reliable for a range of facilities, especially watersports. Wooden chalets have been recently upgraded and new conference facilities make it popular for large meetings. Relax in two pools, a spa and numerous bars and restaurants. 350 rooms.

MELAKA

Puri $$ *118 Jalan Tun Tan Cheng Lock, 75200 Melaka, tel: 06-282 5588, fax: 06-281 5588, www.hotelpuri.com.* Puri is a gem in the historic heart of this heritage city. It was once a narrow 100m (330ft) -long Peranakan house with an open courtyard for circulating the air. Rooms are modern and comfortable and the public areas have museum-quality furnishings. 50 rooms.

Renaissance $$$ *Jalan Bendahara, 75100 Melaka, tel: 06-284 8888, fax: 06-284 92691, www.marriott.com.* A large international hotel within walking distance of the city's historic attractions. The top floor of the 24-storey building is the club lounge with superb views across the town and Strait of Malacca. Contemporary-styled rooms are of international standard and include broadband internet. 294 rooms.

CAMERON HIGHLANDS

Bala's Holiday Chalet $$ *Lot 55 Tanah Rata, 39000 Cameron Highlands, Pahang, tel: 05-491 1660, fax: 05-491 4500, www.bala schalet.com.* This was once a boarding school but is now a small English-styled chalet with a reputation for good-value rooms. Enjoy Devonshire teas, Indian curries and traditional English fare in the restaurant. Take a turn around the gardens and cool down in the mountain air. 30 rooms.

Cameron Highlands Resort $$$$ *by the golf course, 39000 Tanah Rata, Cameron Highlands, Pahang, tel: 05-491 1100, fax: 05-491 1800, www.cameronhighlandsresort.com.* Refined elegance in cool mountain air. The resort recently opened after extensive renovations to a former hotel. It has been decorated along heritage lines but with contemporary facilities. Dine on Japanese cuisine in Gonbei or relax in the Spa Village. 56 rooms.

EAST COAST

Club Med Cherating $$$$ *Batu 29 Jalan Kuantan/Kemaman, 26080 Kuantan, Pahang, tel: 09-581 9133, fax: 09-581 9172, www. clubmed.com.* This 80-hectare (200-acre) east coast resort offers comfortable accommodation in low-rise wooden chalets that reflect the local architecture. Kids' activities are fun, adventurous and well-managed by trained professionals. Suitable for couples or families. All-inclusive packages are available. 297 rooms.

Hyatt Regency Kuantan Resort $$$ *Telok Chempedak, 25050 Kuantan, Pahang, tel: 09-518 1234, fax: 09-567 7577, www. kuantan.regency.hyatt.com.* Appreciate the tranquil east coast from this well-established Hyatt property on the outskirts of Kuantan. The South China Sea laps the easternmost wing of the hotel and guests swim in two pools, dine in three restaurants and relax at sunset in the Sampan Bar (a converted Vietnamese refugee boat). 330 rooms.

KOTA KINABALU

The Magellan Sutera $$$ *1 Sutera Harbour Boulevard, Sutera Harbour, 88100 Kota Kinabalu, Sabah, tel: 088-318 888, fax: 088-303 338, www.suteraharbour.com.* The resort is part of the integrated 155-hectare (383-acre) coastal development of Sutera Harbour, overlooking several islands but minutes from the city. Facilities include a marina, golf course, pools, restaurants, two spas, clubs, bars and luxurious accommodation. 456 rooms.

Shangri-La Tanjung Aru Resort & Spa $$$$ *20 Jalan Aru, 88100 Kota Kinabalu, Sabah, tel: 088-327 888, fax: 088-327 878, www.*

shangri-la.com. Views of the South China Sea don't get much better, especially at sunset. While the beachfront is limited in this expansive resort, five islands are a quick boat trip away. Despite a sense of remoteness, it's just minutes from downtown Kota Kinabalu and the international airport. 492 rooms.

KUCHING

Hilton Kuching $$$ *Jalan Tunku Abdul Rahman, Kuching 93100 Sarawak, tel: 082-248 200, fax: 082-428 984, www.hilton.co.uk/ kuching*. Enjoy majestic views of the Sarawak River and the city's lively waterfront. Relax around the pool or in the fitness centre. Dine in all-day, Chinese or Steakhouse restaurants. Party in Senso Bar or enjoy the club facilities in the executive lounge. 315 rooms.

Telang Usan Hotel $$ *Jalan Ban Hock, 93100 Kuching, Sarawak, tel: 082-415 588, fax: 082-425 316, www.telangusan.com*. Locally owned and operated by Orang Ulu people. Comfortable and well-appointed rooms offer great value for money. Dine on local Dayak cuisine, international dishes and Chinese food at two outlets in the hotel, located just 10 minutes' walk from Kuching's Waterfront. 66 rooms.

MIRI

Miri Marriott Resort & Spa $$$ *Jalan Temenggong Datuk Oyong Lawai, 98000 Miri, Sarawak, tel: 085-421 121, fax: 085-402 855, www.marriott.com/myymc*. The Marriott is the only five-star international hotel in this oil town. Located on the seafront but just minutes from town, it offers superior services and delightfully appointed rooms, mostly with sea views. Zest provides all-day dining. Relax in the Mandara Spa. 220 rooms.

ParkCity Everly Hotel $$ *Jalan Temenggong Datuk Oyong Lawai, 98000 Miri, Sarawak, tel: 085-440 288, fax: 085-419 999, www.vh hotels.com*. Waterfront views and tropical gardens make this a relaxing retreat. Well-appointed rooms, gym and pool provide a resort-like setting. Dine on Malaysian and international favourites in the restaurant and hear live music in the lounge in the evenings. 168 rooms.

Recommended Restaurants

In a nation that lives to eat, no visitor to Malaysia will go hungry. Malaysians are passionate about eating, so food is the country's safest conversational topic. Prices range from the equivalent cost of a cup of coffee in the west for a meal in a Malaysian hawker stall to well up into the stratosphere for dinner in KL's finest restaurants with vintage wines. Visitors will love the range and low prices of simple hawker stalls, take comfort in being able to consume familiar international fast food items and enjoy the selection of near-authentic international cuisines in the larger cities.

Some restaurants serve halal (pork-free) dishes only and possibly no alcohol. International hotels usually serve halal food but with alcohol freely available. Indeed, while not everyone in Malaysia drinks alcohol, it is available in most places and priced without duty on islands such as Langkawi, Labuan and Tioman.

Some restaurants never close while others open for specific meals only. Most Malaysians eat three meals daily but like to snack frequently, so local coffee shops serve drinks and hawker-styled snacks after and in between main meals. Larger establishments accept credit cards but in hawker stalls, it's strictly cash. Many independent restaurants close for one day of the week, usually Monday. Reservations in popular restaurants are recommended.

$$$$	over US$50
$$$	US$25–50
$$	US$10–25
$	less than US$10

KUALA LUMPUR

The Dining Room $$$$ *Carcosa Seri Negara, Taman Tasek Perdana, 50480 Kuala Lumpur, tel: 03-2282 1888.* The Carcosa hotel is something of an institution among the city's social set. Its restaurant allows diners to relive the glamour of the colonial era and enjoy fine contemporary French cuisine with an enticing wine list. The elegant surroundings demand your smartest attire.

Gobo Upstairs $$$ *Traders Hotel Kuala Lumpur, KLCC, 50088 Kuala Lumpur, tel: 03-2332 9888.* A smart contemporary ambience provides a lively and welcoming setting. A limited menu features creative dishes of premium meat cuts from Australia and Argentina. New World wines dominate with an excellent by-the-glass selection.

Jake's $$ *Feast Floor, Starhill Gallery, 161 Jalan Bukit Bintang, 55100 Kuala Lumpur, tel: 03-2148 1398.* Imported steaks cooked to perfection are the speciality at this Wild West-themed restaurant, but the comprehensive menu runs the gamut from seafood to vegetarian dishes. The atmosphere is fun and lively with staff dressed as if they've walked out of a John Wayne movie. The original Jake's is located in suburban Medan Damansara.

La Bodega $$ *Ground Floor, 14–16 Jalan Telawi 2, 59100 Bangsar Baru, tel: 03-2287 8318.* A successful collection of Spanish-inspired restaurants with outlets in all the smart parts of KL. The original Bangsar outlet includes covered pavement dining and a vibrant Mediterranean-themed interior. Expect great paella, tapas and tortillas in a casual setting with a lively bar scene in the evening.

La Terrasse $$ *33 Jalan Berangan, Bukit Bintang, 50250 Kuala Lumpur, tel: 03-2145 4964.* Good, uncomplicated French food in warm surroundings with a semi-open outside bar. Popular with the city's French community, who come for traditional fare rather than fussy nouvelle cuisine. Sunday brunches are popular and great value. There are some excellent pork dishes and the wines are sensibly priced.

Le Bouchon $$$ *14 & 16 Jalan Changkat Bukit Bintang, 50450 Kuala Lumpur, tel: 03-2142 7633.* Run by the same owners as La Terrasse, Le Bouchon is classier but with the same warm ambience and no-nonsense food. The pork-free restaurant maintains a well-heeled clientele who appreciate the great service, wine and food.

Meng Kee $ *13 Tengkat Tong Shin, 50450 Kuala Lumpur.* This stall opens from 11am–2pm and attracts a long queue of hungry diners who come for just two dishes – barbecued pork (supposedly the best in KL) and steamed chicken. Prices are not cheap by KL standards but from a global perspective, dining here is a steal. It's located just around the corner from the famous Jalan Alor food street. Closed on Sundays.

Old China Café $$ *11 Jalan Balai Polis, 50000 Kuala Lumpur, tel: 03-2072 5915.* Eating here is a little like dining in a museum as the walls are lined with photos and memorabilia of the local Chinese laundryman's association. It's one of the city's most atmospheric settings and Chinese (mostly Nyonya) and Asian dishes keep regulars and travellers coming back for more.

Passage Through India $$ *235 Jalan Tun Razak, 55100 Kuala Lumpur, tel: 03-2145 0366.* The 'passage' is set back from the road and a little difficult to see, but for those who drive here there's abundant parking. A comprehensive menu of mostly northern Indian specialities including tandoori and many vegetarian dishes is served in an elaborate setting. The wine list is limited but there are plenty of cold beers and juices to quell the spicy food.

Prime Grill $$$ *11th Floor, Crown Princess Kuala Lumpur, City Square Centre, Jalan Tun Razak, 50400 Kuala Lumpur, tel: 03-2162 5522.* Discreetly overlooking the hotel pool, this elegant place offers glimpses of the Twin Towers. Start with drinks at the bar and move into the subtly-lit restaurant. Expect good food with an emphasis on classic grills, plus a few innovative seafood, pasta and soup offerings. Well chosen and competitively priced wines are a real bonus.

Sao Nam $$ *25 Tengkat Thong Shin, 50200 Kuala Lumpur, tel: 03-2144 8225.* While many Vietnamese food outlets claim authenticity, few have achieved the success of Sao Nam, now with two outlets – KL and suburban Plaza Damas. Trendy diners devour dishes like mangosteen and prawn salad and chicken *pho* (noodle soup). Sao Nam KL is located near the Jalan Alor food street and serves creative food with a well-considered wine list. Closed on Monday.

Senses $$$$ *Hilton Kuala Lumpur, 3 Jalan Stesen Sentral, 50470 Kuala Lumpur, tel: 03-2264 2264.* Senses is guided by Malaysian expatriate and guru of Australian fusion cuisine Cheong Liew. His creative team serves modern Australian cuisine and interpretations of Cheong's signature dishes plus some winners of their own. Dining is a sensory experience and wines are thoughtfully matched with specific dishes. Not cheap, but well worth it.

1885 $$$ *E & O Hotel, 10 Lebuh Farquhar, 10200 Penang, tel: 04-222 2000.* This is the historic and elegant dining room in Penang's famous heritage hotel. Historic hotel devotees make this a 'must-do' dining experience while in Penang. The menu selection is best described as contemporary international with some creative interpretations of seafood and Wagyu beef dishes. A very acceptable wine list complements the food and fine surroundings. Wear your fanciest dress.

Kafe Kheng Pin $ *80 Penang Road/Jalan Sri Bahari, 10200 Penang.* Penang's hawker food is among the best in the country. This stall is within a larger café and various other stalls allow you to make a meal of your visit. Dishes like *lorbak*, which look like spring rolls and are made from soya skin, are superb. Open for breakfast and lunch and closed on Mondays.

Toh Soon Cafe $ *Campbell Street, 10200 Penang.* This is a traditional Chinese coffee shop serving seriously strong coffee, half-boiled eggs, *roti bakar* (toast), *kaya* (sweet spread) and butter. While it's more a covered lane than a café, it's clean and very popular during the day. Closed in the evenings and Sundays.

Gulai House $$$$ *The Andaman, Jalan Teluk Datai, 07000 Langkawi, Kedah, tel: 04-959 1088.* Few restaurants in Malaysia match Gulai House for rustic atmosphere. Enter along the sandy beach of Datai Bay and through pristine coastal rainforest. Diners sit in comfort, surrounded by jungle, and dine on local Malay and Indian favourites. Service is friendly and professional. Wines are an important element of the experience and a well-crafted list is offered. While prices are not cheap, the experience is priceless.

L'Osteria $$$ *Jalan Pantai Tengah, Pantai Tengah, 07100 Langkawi, Kedah, tel: 04-955 2133*. For those pining for pizza, pasta and prosecco, this Italian restaurant dishes up all the popular favourites in comfortable but casual surroundings. Dine in the fan-cooled interior or on the open terrace within a whiff of the salt air coming off the beach. While pizzas are popular, other dishes such as *osso bucco* and tiramisu are a few of Chef Lorenzo's specialities. Some excellent Italian beverages are supported by other international wines.

The Loaf $$ *Perdana Quay, Telaga Harbour Park, Pantai Kok, 07000, Langkawi, Kedah, tel: 04-959 4866*. Overlooking the picturesque flotilla of yachts in the marina, The Loaf serves designer Japanese bakery items, coffees and teas and a selection of more substantial dishes for lunch and dinner. Dine in or take away from morning to late evening.

Nam $$$ *Bon Ton Resort, Pantai Cenang, 07000 Langkawi, Kedah, tel: 04-955 3643*. Island dining doesn't get much better than Nam, located within the designer surroundings of this intimate and stylish resort. Arrive at sunset, enjoy pre-dinner drinks by the lily-lined lagoon and then savour delicious offerings from a menu that changes regularly. Superb wines and friendly, knowledgeable service which makes guests feel like they have been part of the furniture forever.

Unkaizan $$$ *Jalan Telok Baru, Pantai Tengah, 07100 Langkawi, Kedah, tel: 04-955 4118*. Enjoy excellent Japanese cuisine in a remote part of the island near the Star Cruise Terminal. Dine outside, downstairs or on Japanese-styled seating upstairs. Expect the freshest seafood live from an in-restaurant tank. Most popular Japanese cooking styles are available and there's a respectable wine and *sake* selection.

MELAKA

Hoe Kee Chicken Rice Shop $ *4 Jalan Hang Jebat (Jonkers Street), 72500 Melaka, tel: 06-283 4751*. Melaka is famous for its chicken rice and this is considered one of the best in the city. The business has been going for over half a century and the formula is popular with diners from all over the country. Dine on steamed chicken, rice balls, Assam fish curry and lotus root soup. Open from morning to late afternoon.

Sun May Hiong Satay House ('Jonker Satay') $ *50/50A Jalan Kota Laksamana 1/1, Taman Kota Laksaman, 72500, Melaka.* Satay is one of the favourite local dishes, freshly barbecued over charcoal. Enjoy succulent meat and a 'special' peanut sauce. Open from 11am to 6pm (8pm on Saturdays) but closed on alternate Tuesdays.

CAMERON HIGHLANDS

Gonbei $$$$ *Cameron Highlands Resort, 39000 Tanah Rata, Cameron Highlands, Pahang, tel: 05-491 1100.* This open-sided, Zen-like structure faces gardens of bamboo. The food is excellent with input from chefs in the Starhill Gallery outlet in KL. Enjoy a wide selection of *sakes* and try the *bento* sets for a range of Japanese delicacies.

Restoran Sheng Ming $ *18 Main Road, Tanah Rata, 39000 Cameron Highlands, Pahang, tel: 05-491 2143.* Go local in the highlands and enjoy some no-nonsense Hainanese Chinese food. Choose from chicken chops, fried rice and fried noodles in this popular coffee shop. Open daily from 8am to 7pm.

EAST COAST

Nelayan $$$ *Tanjong Jara Resort, Batu 8, off Jalan Dungan, 23000 Dungan, Terengganu, tel: 09-845 1100.* East coast elegance steeped in cultural heritage with some of the coast's freshest seafood. Most dishes are prepared and cooked using traditional spices and methods. Pasta, lamb and beef dishes are also available. Enjoy the magical and tranquil setting by the sea.

KOTA KINABALU

@mosphere Modern Dining $$$$ *18th Floor, Menara Tun Mustapha, Jalan Sulaman, 88859 Kota Kinabalu, Sabah, tel: 088-425 100.* Enjoy fantastic views of coastal Sabah from this revolving restaurant. Expect designer chic in the decor and Pacific Rim in the food. New World wines dominate an excellent wine list. This becomes the funkiest place in KK to meet and drink later in the evening. Impress your friends and arrive by helicopter – restaurant staff will make the arrangements.

Hinompuka Café $ *Lot 7, Block F, SED-O Shophouses, Buhavan Square, Donggongon New Township, 88300 Panampang, tel: 088-725 996.* Enjoy some local Kadazan cuisine including dishes like *hinava* (raw fish cooked in lime juice) and various local vegetables. This is mostly a breakfast and lunch place and food is served buffet-style. Helpful staff will explain the dishes. Closed on Sundays.

KUCHING

Chong Choon Café $ *Jalan Abell, 93000 Kuching, Sarawak.* Sarawakians don't eat here for the surroundings or ambience, but this simple café supposedly serves the best Sarawak *laksa* in the world. The broth is made from coconut milk and spices and has a sour taste. Noodles, omelette strips and prawns complete the dish. Be prepared to queue and don't come late – there won't be any left. Open daily from 6.30am to 2pm.

The Steakhouse $$$ *Hilton Kuching, Jalan Tunku Abdul Rahman, 93100 Kuching, Sarawak, tel: 082-248 200.* This smart restaurant has pleasant river views from the window tables and the international menu satisfies the palates of discerning diners. Grilled meat dishes feature but there are also selections of seafood, lamb and prawns. The service is friendly and helpful and there is a good wine list too.

MIRI

Zest $$$ *Miri Marriott Resort & Spa, Jalan Temenggong Datuk Oyong Lawai, 98000 Miri, Sarawak, tel: 085-421 121.* Zest has been recently remodelled to offer a lively and exciting way of presenting food. The open kitchen enables lots of chef-guest interaction. Breakfast and lunch buffets are excellent and these are also available in the evening on most weekends. Enjoy Asian and Italian favourites including freshly made pizza.

INDEX